Extreme Crafts
for Messy Churches

The Bible Reading Fellowship
15 The Chambers, Vineyard
Abingdon OX14 3FE
brf.org.uk

The Bible Reading Fellowship (BRF) is a Registered Charity (233280)
The **Messy Church®** name and logo are registered trade marks of BRF

ISBN 978 0 85746 973 1
First published 2015
This edition published 2021
10 9 8 7 6 5 4 3 2 1 0
All rights reserved

The authors assert the moral right to be identified as the author of this work

Acknowledgements
Unless otherwise acknowledged, scripture quotations are taken from The Holy
Bible, New International Version (Anglicised edition) copyright © 1979, 1984, 2011
by Biblica. Used by permission of Hodder & Stoughton Publishers, a Hachette
UK company. All rights reserved. 'NIV' is a registered trademark of Biblica. UK
trademark number 1448790.

Scripture quotations marked CEV are taken from the Contemporary English
Version. New Testament © American Bible Society 1991, 1992, 1995. Old Testament
© American Bible Society 1995. Anglicisations © British & Foreign Bible Society
1996. Used by permission.

Every effort has been made to trace and contact copyright owners for material
used in this resource. We apologise for any inadvertent omissions or errors, and
would ask those concerned to contact us so that full acknowledgement can be
made in the future.

A catalogue record for this book is available from the British Library

Printed and bound by CPI Group (UK) Ltd, Croydon CR0 4YY

Extreme Crafts
for Messy Churches

80 ACTIVITY IDEAS
FOR THE ADVENTUROUS

**Barry Brand and
Pete Maidment**

Barry:

For Adele, George, Freddie
and my amazing extended Bitterne Messy family.
You guys are awesome.

Pete:

For Jolly and Moshua.

Contents

Construction crafts

Science crafts

Arty crafts

Edible crafts

Appendix

Acknowledgement

There are some people who leave an everlasting mark on your life. Helen Copsey was one. It was a surprise when Helen offered to be on the team at the new Bitterne Messy Church. We went to different services, so I'd never seen her before. She told me she'd done various church stuff before and had always been in the kitchen. But she didn't want to be in the kitchen this time: she wanted to be out with the families.

Helen was put in charge of our edible crafts table and had quite a surprise when 150 people turned up to our first Messy session. She was too ill to help at the next two, but she still brought cakes for the lunch before going home.

Helen didn't really let on just how ill she was and, very sadly, she passed away. The last time I saw her was at one of Pete's Messy training events. She was so excited, desperately wanting to get back to our Messy Church and share the love of Jesus with the families by simply decorating cakes and biscuits and chatting.

Thank you, Helen, for sharing your love and faith. You made your mark and the edible crafts table, 'Copsey's corner', is still the most popular.

Barry

Introduction

'The trouble with Messy Church is that it isn't really for men, is it?'

You would be amazed how often we hear this opinion. Every time you get a bunch of people together to discuss Messy Church or to consider launching a new one somewhere, someone will make this statement.

This is a bit strange, because the two of us are, not to put too fine a point on it, men. We're both in excess of six feet tall. Between us we've run marathons, climbed mountains and built stuff. We both drink beer and eat curry and, at the time of writing, we're having a beard-growing competition, which Barry is winning hands down – Pete's scraggly, patchy, mostly ginger growth can't really be called a beard. Since writing and a few years down the line (2020), Barry is blessed with a fine beard of 6 inches in length; Pete, not so much.

Perhaps the assumption that people make when they announce that Messy Church isn't for men is that once a month we set all that to one side and, with the mums, grannies and childminders (female), we get down to some fancy, pretty, arty-crafty activities with the children.

It simply isn't true.

We need to tread carefully here, because we're at risk of creating all sorts of stereotypical and unhelpful gender divides. Girls, boys, men and women are all capable of doing the same things and enjoying similar activities when it comes to Messy Church. Boys' activities don't have to involve guns and girls' activities don't demand glitter. Men are just as likely to enjoy careful, fiddly craft activities as women are to enjoy boisterous physical activity.

I guess the difference is that men are unlikely to want to be perceived as taking part in crafty stuff. That's why it's called 'Messy' Church, not 'Crafty' Church, and why the first hour is spent at 'activity' tables rather than 'craft' tables.

This book, then, isn't a list of crafts for men, and it's not a list of men's activities. Rather, it's a selection of some of the more extreme activities that we've had a go at in our Messy Churches, which have given us real enjoyment. Above all, though, it's a list of things for you to do, as adults and children together, to try something new and to learn about following Jesus in this crazy world we live in.

We've carefully chosen activities that fit some of those harder-to-fill areas at Messy Church. Our science experiments build on people's natural desire to solve problems and understand things: they're messy and fun, but they stretch the imagination too, expecting us to think outside the box to see how something is done or how it works.

We've included a list of 'big stuff' – activities that call for people to work together to make something bigger than they could manage alone. Which of us didn't don a hard hat as a child and head out to build something?

Food has universal appeal, but our recipes (if you can call them that) are about creating great stuff to eat rather than using food as a craft.

We've also included a section on art and craft, but possibly not as you've imagined it before. Whether it's just a teeny bit dangerous, extra messy or just BIG, these ideas will, we hope, appeal to every-one – even the men!

Big stuff

Toy car track

Mess rating 2/5 • Danger rating 3/5 • Difficulty 5/5

I haven't met many children or dads who don't like toy cars. I'm sure such people must exist, but in this craft it's as much to do with the ingenuity and problem-solving as with the little toy car.

This junk craft is quite simple in theory. All you need to do is get the car from one end of the room to the other with one push, not allowing it to travel on the floor. When we did this at our Messy Church, I'm not sure who had the most fun, kids or dads. We spent a whole hour on it and only managed a perfect run a couple of times. (Some quick repairs were needed when a toddler rampaged Godzilla-like through the middle of the track.)

Themes

Perseverance; Christian journey

Craft outline

You will need

- A Hot Wheels™ car or similar toy car with good, straight wheels
- Various junk items: card, tubes, boxes, pipe, foam and so on
- String; sticky tape; scissors

Depending on the size of your room, you need to start your track high enough to give the car momentum but not so high that the car just flies off before the end. Use whatever comes to hand – chairs, pews, microphone stands – but be careful not to damage any paintwork.

Talk about

- Our journey through life can be difficult at times, but, with perseverance and faith, we can overcome the obstacles in our way
- Have you ever thought of your life as a journey with ups (good times) and downs (bad times)?

Fruit catapult

Mess rating 4/5 • Danger rating 3/5 • Difficulty 4/5

This activity is something of a legend at the St Wilfrid's Messy Church. When someone said, 'Do you think we could make a catapult for firing fruit?', we didn't realise quite what we had let ourselves in for.

Themes

Fruit of the Spirit; evangelism; good news

Craft outline

You will need

- Pieces of wood (sizes roughly as shown in the diagram: all measurements are in centimetres)
- Hammer and nails
- Thick, strong elastic
- Old, soft fruit; a plastic bowl or cup

The catapult shown in the diagram below is a bit like a trebuchet, with a heavy wooden base, an arm at the top that pivots on a wooden support, and a cup to load the fruit into. For the elastic, we would recommend using a giant elastic band from a physiotherapist, if available.

At its simplest, you could get away with two stakes hammered into the ground, with the elastic tied on to the tops. You can then load the fruit up, pull back the elastic and let it fly.

Whatever design you choose to go with, make sure you test it before use, work out where it's safe to stand, and so on. There's nothing more disappointing than setting up a catapult, only to discover that your fruit will fly barely a few feet.

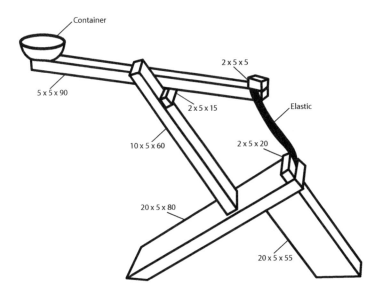

To download the diagram, go to **messychurch.org.uk/extremecrafts**

Once you're all set up, preferably outdoors with plenty of space, let people take turns in loading up some fruit and seeing who can fire it the furthest. You can compare different fruits or different loading and aiming techniques, to turn it into a really geeky science experiment, if you like.

Talk about

- How much fun is it to spread the fruit around the churchyard?
- Have you got a message you'd love to share?
- The Bible says that spiritual fruit can grow in us (see Galatians 5:22–23). What kinds of 'fruit' do you think God might give us to bless us?
- Why does God want us to share the good news rather than keep it to ourselves?

Junk whale

Mess rating 3/5 • Danger rating 2/5 • Difficulty 3/5

This craft causes a lot of excitement. Young children love the finished whale because they can get inside it, and the adults and older children love the challenge of building it. We made a blow-hole in our whale and I finished off my talk with my head sticking out of the top.

Theme

Jonah and the big fish

Craft outline

You will need

- Bendy bamboo sticks or the poles from a two-pole play tent
- Wire coat hangers
- Black bin bags; dust sheets or bed sheets
- Paper; sticky tape

Use the bamboo sticks or play tent poles to form the main body of the whale. Use more bamboo or wire coat hangers to form the tail and fins. Cover the structure with the bin bags and sheets and decorate to look as whale-like as possible. Some of the smaller children might like to make some paper barnacles or seaweed to stick to the whale.

Try to make a mouth that opens and closes, so that you can go inside.

Talk about

- Have you ever done something wrong and tried to hide it or forget about it? Can we hide from God?
- God wants us to tell him about our wrongdoings and ask him for forgiveness, for help and for strength to face our fears
- Have you ever played hide and seek? Hiding from God isn't much fun
- Sometimes God or our parents can ask us to do things we don't want to do. This happened to Jonah
- Have you ever been too scared to do the right thing?

Giant Jenga™

Mess rating 1/5 • Danger rating 3/5 • Difficulty 2/5

This is a big build that takes the pub garden game to another level. You can have lots of fun building your tower to see how high you can get it and then taking it down again, box by box. Either make one tower or split into teams and make two or more.

Themes

> **The tower of Babel** (Genesis 11:1–9); **the wise and foolish builders** (Matthew 7:24–27); **being God's building** (Ephesians 2:19–22; 1 Corinthians 3:9)

Craft outline

You will need

- Cardboard boxes of different sizes; parcel tape

Tape your boxes closed so that they are nice and square, and start building up a tower from the floor. Use a mixture of big and small boxes, interlocking them to add strength, like a dry-stone wall.

Then try removing boxes without letting the whole tower collapse. The more boxes you use to build it up, the better your game of Jenga™ will be.

Talk about

- How can we help God build his church?
- How can we grow stronger in our faith?

Walking on eggs

Mess rating 1/5 (unless it goes wrong, in which case it's 5/5) • Danger rating 3/5 • Difficulty 2/5

This is a totally unbelievable activity. All the children will want to have a go, and the dads will want to try to work out how it's done. A raw, unbroken egg is incredibly strong when standing upright, so a box of six can easily support a child's (and even an adult's) weight.

Themes

Faith and trust; walking on water (Matthew 14:22–33)

Craft outline

You will need

- Several boxes of eggs in their boxes (six boxes will allow six steps, but you may want some spares. Most of the eggs will remain usable at the end of the activity)
- A plastic sheet to put on the ground, if you are of little faith

Place the boxes of eggs on the ground, spread out so that people can step from one box to the next. It's probably best done without shoes and socks, and you may want to walk alongside the volunteer, holding their hand for balance.

If anyone doubts that the eggs are real, invite them to stand on just one, laid on its side, to prove you're not lying.

Talk about

- Do you trust that the eggs will hold your weight? Why/why not?
- Is it easy to put our trust in Jesus?
- How do we know that God will look after us?

Collapsing house

Mess rating 2/5 • Danger rating 2/5 • Difficulty 3/5

This is a great junk craft that sounds simple at first but can get very technical, depending on how you decide to make it collapse. We used it when we talked about the wise and foolish builders. (This, obviously, is the house that the foolish man built on the sand.)

Build the house large enough to be used in the talk, with the speaker inside when it collapses.

Theme

> **The wise and foolish builders** (Matthew 7:24–27)

Craft outline

You will need

- Corrugated cardboard; string; scissors; sticky tape; pens; crayons

Using corrugated cardboard, make four separate sides and a roof that will hold up to being knocked without collapsing before you want it to. Make a door to get in at and a window to look out of while you tell the story of the two builders.

Hold the walls together with small bits of tape, and tie string to each corner at the top of the inside walls. Whoever is inside can then pull the strings and literally bring the house down.

Children love decorating and building the house. Dads love coming up with the most ingenious ways to collapse it.

Talk about

- The Bible story of the two builders and what it means
- Working together

Bubble snakes

Mess rating 5/5 • Danger rating 1/5 • Difficulty 2/5

Bubbles seem to appeal to all ages. The bigger the better, the more the merrier and, in this activity, the longer the better. If you do this activity inside, you might produce longer bubbles; outside, if it's a bit windy, you'll be able to have them sailing away.

Themes

> **The Holy Spirit; Moses' and Aaron's staff** (Exodus 4:1–5; 7:8–13); **prayer** (Matthew 7:7–12); **the garden of Eden** (Genesis 3:1–13)

Craft outline

You will need

- Plastic bottles of any size; flannels; scissors; elastic bands; washing-up liquid; water; bowl

Cut the bottom off a plastic bottle (but keep the neck end). Cut the flannel down to a size that will fit over the cut part of the bottle and attach it with an elastic band. Mix up some washing-up liquid and water in the bowl and dip the bottle in, flannel side down.

Blow (*don't suck*) down through the neck end to create a foam snake
made out of tiny bubbles (a bit like bubble bath). You may need to
adjust the ratio of washing-up liquid to water to get it perfect, but,
if you do it correctly, you can make snakes over five feet long.

Add even more interest to this activity by dotting the flannel with
different food colourings before dipping it in the bubble mix, to get
rainbow bubble snakes.

Talk about

- Have you ever held a snake?
- The serpent in the garden of Eden
- Why are some people scared of snakes?

Giant rain sticks

Mess rating 3/5 • Danger rating 4/5 • Difficulty 4/5

We've all played with rain sticks, and you might even have made rain sticks in a craft session, but these giant versions take some beating. You are limited only by the length of your carpet tubes. Can you imagine a five-metre-long rain stick?

Themes

> **Noah** (Genesis 6—9); **Jesus calming the storm** (Luke 8:22–25); **creation; water; music**

Craft outline

You will need

- Cardboard carpet-roll tubes; chicken wire; tin snips
- Newspaper; packing tape; gravel; scoop
- Strong gloves; saw

In advance, you will need to saw your carpet tubes into roughly metre-long sections and, using the tin snips, cut the chicken wire into pieces of a similar length. The chicken wire will be quite spiky, so be careful.

With an adult, and wearing the gloves, roll the chicken wire tightly enough to be stuffed inside the carpet tubes. This is tricky: you'll need to feed it in carefully from one end and reach inside the tube to pull it through from the other. Be aware of how sharp the ends of the chicken wire are, and make sure that parents and children alike are careful not to hurt themselves.

Once the wire is well inside the tube, use newspaper and packing tape to cover one end of your rain stick. When it's secure, pour a scoopful of gravel in through the open end. Then seal the top of the tube with more paper and packing tape.

Tip the rain stick up and listen to the gravel trickling through the wire. You can decorate the rain sticks if you like.

Talk about

- What does the noise from the stick remind you of?
- Have you ever been in a storm? How did it feel?
- Do you think God keeps us safe when we're scared?
- Jesus once offered someone 'living water' (John 4:10). What do you think he meant?

Fossil hunting

Mess rating 4/5 • Danger rating 3/5 • Difficulty 2/5

Anything vaguely dinosaur-related is bound to catch the interest of boys at your Messy Church, so digging for fossils, rocks and dinosaur bones should be a real crowd-pleaser.

Themes

Exploring the world; Nicodemus investigating Jesus (John 3:1–14)

Craft outline

You will need

- Large metal oven trays; water or plaster of Paris
- Toy dinosaurs; rocks; small action figures (Moshi Monsters™ would work well)
- Hammers; chisels (the kind for breaking up stones or bricks, not wood chisels)
- Goggles; heavy-duty gloves

A good couple of days in advance, fill the trays with water and drop in the various rocks, dinosaurs and action figures. Then put the trays in the freezer to freeze.

At your Messy Church session, dig out the toys with the hammers and chisels. If you really want to go to town, why not set the toys in plaster of Paris rather than ice? It'll be a whole lot messier and much more authentic.

Talk about

- What do you think you'll find in the tray?
- How determined are you to discover what's hidden?
- Why do you think people like Nicodemus were so keen to find out about Jesus?

Cardboard mountain

Mess rating 3/5 • Danger rating 3/5 • Difficulty 3/5

Like many of the others, this craft can be used in the talk later on, in this case to make your very own sermon on the mount. To the untrained eye it looks a mess, but a lot of thought is needed in the construction if you want to build a big mountain. Watching dads plan and work together seriously on the construction of a massive cardboard mountain is priceless.

Theme

Sermon on the Mount (Matthew 5—7)

Craft outline

You will need

- Lots of cardboard packaging and corrugated card; large sheets of grey paper; black bin bags
- Glue; sticky tape
- Stepladder with handle rail in front

Make a mountain out of whatever junk you have.

The stepladder is important as you need to be able to stand safely at the top of it to give a talk at the end.

Take large pieces of cardboard packaging, together with more thick corrugated card, and stick it all together around the stepladder in a mountain shape. Try to hide the ladder completely by making the mountain quite wide at the bottom and bringing it around the sides of the ladder. Add screwed-up grey paper and bin bags to the front to make it more textured. If you want, you could even paint it.

The bigger the mountain, the more impressed everyone will be at talk time.

Talk about

- Do you sometimes struggle to get people to listen to you?
- When Jesus gave one of his most important set of teachings, he went up a hill so that everyone could hear him. Jesus is for everyone, he is everywhere and God hears every prayer
- Everything Jesus said was important as a guide to how we should live

Noah's ark and creatures

Mess rating 2/5 • Danger rating 0/5 • Difficulty 2/5

This is a great junk craft – to build a big ark and creatures to go on it. I say 'creatures' because, with the junk we had lying about, not everything we made looked like normal animals.

Themes

Noah's ark (Genesis 6—9); **new beginnings; God gives us another chance when we mess up**

Craft outline

You will need

- Corrugated cardboard; cardboard boxes
- Parcel tape; scissors; glue; paint
- Various junk items (pipe cleaners, foam, small plastic bottles, wool, foil, pegs and so on)

Using the cardboard, make a large ark with different floors, ramps, steps, and maybe even with opening sides like a doll's house, so that you can see what's going on inside. Really go for it with the design: don't just stick boxes together.

With all the other junk, make some creatures to live on the ark. Let your imagination go wild!

Talk about

- Any recent examples of flooding in your country/area
- All the different kinds of animals in the world
- How water can be fun but also, at times, scary
- How hard it would have been for Noah to build the ark by hand with no power tools
- What would life have been like on the ark? Noisy, smelly, uncomfortable, boring, scary?
- Why is it so hard to wait for something? Noah had to have faith and be patient for a long time
- The rainbow and God's promise not to flood the earth again. God never breaks his promises

Sticky fishing net game

Mess rating 2/5 • Danger rating 1/5 • Difficulty 2/5

This activity is more about the game at the end than the build, but, as quick as the build is, it's a lot of fun to do. It really draws out the competitive streak in the adults as well as the kids.

Themes

> **Jesus' miraculous catch of fish** (John 21:1–14); **Jesus calls four fishermen** (Mark 1:14–20); **the parable of the net** (Matthew 13:47–50); **God provides for us if we pray**

Craft outline

You will need

- Masking tape; newspaper

Use the masking tape to make a diamond pattern net across a doorway, sticking the ends to the door frame. Screw up the newspaper into balls (to represent little fish). The idea is to get your fish to stick to the tape, so the bigger the holes, the harder the game will be.

Mark a line on the floor and stand at it as you take turns to throw your fish at the sticky net. You can ramp up the competition element by marking a target on the tape.

Talk about

- Have you ever been fishing?
- Do you talk to your friends about Jesus?
- What does it mean to 'fish for people' (Mark 1:17)?

Circus skills

Mess rating 1/5 • Danger rating 4/5 • Difficulty 5/5

This is not really a craft, but you can take it one step further and make your own circus equipment. We run this activity for the children who don't always want to do a craft. There could well be a member of your church who is a secret juggler; if not, then get practising before you start.

We bought some spinning plates, diabolos and beanbags for juggling from **oddballs.co.uk**, which produces packs and individual items for workshops. It's great to see children and adults alike trying something for the first time on a level playing field, and even better when you see the kids improving their skills faster than their parents.

Theme

Perseverance

Craft outline

You will need

- Balls and/or bean bags
- Plastic spinning plates

- Diabolos
- Flower sticks

It can be expensive to buy all this equipment; we also run a circus skills workshop during the week so that it gets plenty of use. If your budget allows, go for it; if not, you can easily make or improvise some of the equipment. Use tennis balls or something similar for juggling. You could make flower sticks with some dowel and small pieces of ribbon (search for images on the internet if necessary).

Talk about

- Not giving up when something seems too hard
- Gifts
- Teaching

Tumbling walls

Mess rating 2/5 • **Danger rating 3/5** • **Difficulty 2/5**

This activity is so much fun for young and old alike. It's simple to do and worth the time finding as many boxes as you can. Some will get their fun out of building, but if you're anything like me, you'll get the most enjoyment knocking it down.

Themes

Walls of Jericho (Joshua 6); **rebuilding the walls of Jerusalem** (Nehemiah 3); **the wise and foolish builders** (Matthew 7:24–27)

Craft outline

You will need

- Lots of cardboard boxes of different sizes
- Parcel tape
- Old socks or bean bags

Start by taping the boxes closed so they're nice and rigid. The more boxes you have the better, as you need to build a long and tall wall. For some, this will be the best bit, getting it nice and square and strong with all the different shapes interlinking. If you have bean bags, great, but if not use a bunch of old socks rolled up and stuffed inside each other. Mark a line a distance away from the wall and throw the socks at the wall to try and knock it down. Have different throwing distances for different ages.

Talk about

- How we should build people up and help them when they get knocked down
- How can have strength in Jesus?
- How can help God build his church?

Fishers of men

Mess rating 4/5 • **Danger rating 2/5** • **Difficulty 3/5**

We have done this a small individual prayer craft, but this just lends itself to being a really cool big prayer craft activity. Depending on the skills of your team, you could even make a wooden boat. Maybe you have a retired carpenter or handyman in your congregation you could ask to help.

Themes

Jesus calls four fishermen (Mark 1:14–20); **the parable of the net** (Matthew 13:47–50); **the miraculous catch of fish** (John 21:1–6)

Craft outline

You will need

- Cardboard
- Paper
- String
- Scissors/craft knife
- Sticky tape and glue
- Colouring pens, pencils, paint

Build a simple rowboat out of the cardboard. If you have the team, it would be awesome to build this out of wood. Go as big as you want, can or are able to display. When the boat is built, you can then decorate it. Draw some people on some more cardboard and cut them out so they can sit in the boat. Once they're done, draw and cut out some fish shapes on some more cardboard. Attach the fish to the string and the string to the side of the boat. Write the names of Christians you know on to the people, so they can be prayed for as they go out and spread God's message of love. Write the names of people you know who you want to hear the message of God's love on to the fish.

Talk about

- How could we fish for people?
- Do you talk to your friends about Jesus?
- Have you ever rowed a boat or been fishing?
- Fisherman use bait to catch fish. What bait would you use to catch people?

Giant marble run

Mess rating 3/5 • Danger rating 2/5 • Difficulty 4/5

Marble runs are great to make and fun to play with. But what's better than a marble run? A giant marble run! Another great activity for all ages, but the dad's always get very involved in this one, with awesome over-complicated designs.

Themes

The narrow gate (Matthew 6:13–24); **journeys** (for example, the road to Emmaus, Damascus, Abraham in the desert); **the widow's offering** (Mark 12:41–44); **following Jesus**

Craft outline

You will need

- Marbles
- Junk – cardboard, tubes, boxes, string, etc.
- Scissors
- Tape and or glue

Stick some heavy-duty card together to form your back and stand it up against a wall. Now with all the different junk you have collected, create a run from the top to the bottom. You could do a simple zig zag or go really creative. Build bridges, tunnels or crazy swinging mechanisms. You're only limited by your imagination!

Talk about

- Sometimes it's not the destination but the journey that's important
- Have you ever been on a long journey or adventure?
- What's it like to follow Jesus?

Where we live

Mess rating 3/5 · Danger rating 2/5 · Difficulty 3/5

In our communities we are all different and so are the places where we live: houses, semi, detached, terraced, bungalows, flats, apartments, etc. And then there are the shops we visit and the pubs and the church and the schools. This is a great way of bringing everyone together and feeling more like a family where we see all the things we have in common.

Themes

God among us (Matthew 18:20); **a city on a hill** (Matthew 5:13–16); **living in peace** (Psalm 133)

Craft outline

You will need

- Card
- Scissors
- Glue and or tape
- Felt-tip pens or paint
- Tracing paper
- Battery tea lights

Draw the front of your home on to the card, adding as much detail as you can remember. Now carefully with the scissors or a craft knife cut out the windows and then stick the tracing paper over the windows on the inside. Stick a little bit of folded card on the back so it will stand up. Now do the same with the other buildings in your community like shops, pubs, cafes, church and schools. Set up a display to show off all the different buildings and put a battery tea light behind each of the buildings. The glow will shine through all of the windows. This would be a great end to a Messy Church where you can turn off the main lights so just the tea lights are on and pray for your community.

Make sure you use battery tea lights and not real ones.

Talk about

- Where do you live?
- How many shops can you name where you live? Which is your favourite?
- How many people live with you?
- Jesus used to stay in different people's houses. How would you feel if he wanted to stay with you?
- Would you like to be happy in a shed or sad in a mansion?

Pallet wood signs

Mess rating 4/5 • Danger rating 4/5 • Difficulty 3/5

Inspirational quote signs seem to be all the rage at the moment. Here is an activity to make your own using quotes from the Bible. This is another great activity to show children how to use tools and be safe. Make sure to have enough team to help at this one for safety.

Themes

The leaders demand a miraculous sign (Matthew 16); **signs, messages**

Craft outline

You will need

- Pallet wood (you can find this at wood rec places already dismantled or off of places like Facebook Marketplace. Be careful of nails and splinters if you are taking them apart yourself).
- Saw
- Sandpaper
- Wood screws (slightly smaller than two boards stacked on top of each other)
- Battery screwdriver

- Jute or sisal rope around 8mm thick
- Large nibbed paint pens
- Watered down poster paint

If your pallets are whole, break them apart before the session into individual planks. You can then saw them down to size or get the families to do that and teach them to saw as well. Lengths of around 45 cm are good. Use the sandpaper to remove any rough bits.

Lay three lengths of wood down on the floor next to each other, making a rectangle roughly 45 cm x 30 cm. Cut another two lengths about 20–25 cm long and screw them down on the back side of the three boards towards each end to join them together. Tie a length of the rope around the top screw at each end before screwing them down tight. This will be used for hanging your sign up. Now turn the sign over to the front. Using the paint pens, write your Bible quote. It might be a good idea to have some Bibles out, as well as some quote ideas and some examples of lettering styles for people to try and copy. Once the writing is dry (it won't take long), brush over the watered-down paint like a stain over the wood for some colour.

Talk about

- What things do you think Jesus made as a carpenter?
- Who does the DIY at home? Do you help?
- Signs can tell us important messages or information. What signs can you see in this building?

Trust boxes

Mess rating 4/5 • Danger rating 1/5 • Difficulty 2/5

This activity was inspired by the TV show *I'm a Celebrity… Get Me Out of Here!* You could make smaller individual sets to take home, but I think it's more fun to make three large ones which can then be used in your talk. I have used mine many times at various services and assemblies, not just Messy Church. This isn't delicate fine art. These need to be as gross as you can get them. They are great to use in a talk about trust, getting up some children or, better yet, parents and seeing if they trust you enough to put their hands in the boxes. Depending on your talk you can put goodies inside or yukky stuff, whatever works – just have fun with it. For max effect, build up the tension, pretend you've forgotten which is the good box and which is the bad.

Themes

Trust; fear; faith; bravery; courage

Craft outline

You will need

- Three identical cardboard boxes with flaps intact for lid (rough size 30cm x 30 cm x 40 cm is ideal)

- Paint
- PVA glue
- Plastic (a thick carrier bag works well)
- Craft knife

Seal each box up making them nice and strong. Take the craft knife and cut a circle in the middle of the top of each of the boxes big enough to squeeze a hand into. Now bash the corners up a bit being careful to not destroy the boxes. You want them to look old and battered. Mix your various paints with some of the PVA glue and paint all over the boxes. The PVA will help strengthen the boxes and give them a little shine. You want to make them look really horrible and unpleasant. Go overboard with this and let your imagination run wild. The glue will help it look wet and slimy even when it is dry. When you've finished painting, glue a slightly larger circle of plastic over the hole on top and cut a slit down the middle so you can't see in when you put your hand in.

Talk about

- What things frighten you?
- Who do you trust?
- Putting your trust in Jesus
- Good and bad choices, consequences

Construction crafts

Cocktail sticks and peas

Mess rating 1/5 • Danger rating 3/5 • Difficulty 4/5

This is for the dads and kids who love construction toys such as Meccano or Knex. The only limit is your own imagination. We've used sticks and peas to build pyramids and a large temple – and with a Messy Church of over 150 people, this craft cost less than £2.

Themes

> **The temple; the tower of Babel** (Genesis 11:1–9); **the wise and foolish builders** (Matthew 7:24–27); **creation**

Craft outline

You will need

- A few packs of cocktail sticks
- A box of dried marrowfat peas (soaked for about twelve hours and drained)
- Sticky tack or Plasticine

It's important to soak the dried peas overnight before your Messy Church, or it just won't work.

All you need to do is put a pea on the end of a cocktail stick, put another cocktail stick into the same pea, and carry on connecting the sticks in the same way. You can build a simple pyramid with six sticks and four peas; keep going and you can build a tower of Babel. When the peas dry out again, they will strengthen the whole structure.

If you are doing this activity on a table, perhaps building a large construction like a temple, use the sticky tack or Plasticine to secure the bottom of the structure to the table. This will strengthen it and stop it from slipping.

Talk about

- How do you think big temples were built in Jesus' time and before?
- Can you speak another language?
- Have you gone on holiday to another country?
- What would your dream house look like, and how many rooms do you really need?
- How can you build your life on firm foundations with the help of God?

Clothes peg catapults

Mess rating 2/5 • Danger rating 3/5 • Difficulty 3/5

Anything that fires anything anywhere is always popular. These little catapults are fiddly but the final result looks good and can be great fun to play with (but don't ping stuff into people's faces). Follow the instructions below or do an internet search for 'clothes peg catapults' for further inspiration.

Themes

Mission; mountains; Jesus' ascension (Luke 24:50–53)

Craft outline

You will need

* Wooden clothes pegs; elastic bands; plastic spoons; pre-cut wooden bases

Position your clothes peg on the wooden base, so that the top (the bit you squeeze) is level with one end of the block. Secure it tightly with two elastic bands, one at each end (see diagram).

Place your plastic spoon on top of the clothes peg and secure it with two further elastic bands. This is the really fiddly bit and will need you to wrap the bands round several times.

Now load the spoon up and ping away. You could compete to see how far people can fire things, or you could have a selection of materials available so that people can come up with their own catapult designs. Encourage some engineering at your Messy Church!

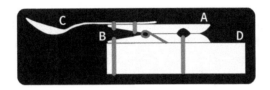

Key

A Clothes peg   B Elastic band
C Plastic spoon D Wooden block

To download the diagram, go to **messychurch.org.uk/extremecrafts**

Talk about

- How far can you catapult your projectiles?
- How can we share the good news about Jesus?
- What do you think 'Jesus was taken up into heaven' means?
- How do you think the disciples felt about being left behind?

Tin can star lamp

Mess rating 2/5 • Danger rating 5/5 • Difficulty 4/5

This lamp looks really cool when it's finished. When it's lit, the nail holes look like stars and will make patterns on the table, too. You could make several lamps in different sizes. Use a battery-operated tea light if the lamp is to be used in a child's room.

Themes

Creation; the star of Bethlehem; angels

Craft outline

You will need

- Empty food tins (use an opener that doesn't leave sharp edges: tins with a ring-pull lid are best)
- Hammer; nail; foam or sliced-up discs of cork from wine bottles; PVA glue
- Tealights or battery-operated tea lights

Make sure that your opened tins don't have sharp edges. With your hammer and nail, carefully pierce holes randomly all over the tin (except for the bottom). Stick four cork or foam discs to the bottom of the tin with the PVA glue. Place the tea light inside.

Talk about

- All the stars in the sky
- God's people shining like stars
- Jesus, the light of the world

Squawking cans

Mess rating 2/5 • Danger rating 3/5 • Difficulty 3/5

These tin-can 'musical instruments' make the most horrendous noise. It's great fun making any kind of musical instrument, and these feel good and industrial, especially when you use a hammer and nail to punch the hole in the can. Be warned: parents will hate you for allowing their children to make them!

Themes

Music; Psalm 150

Craft outline

You will need

- Clean empty tins or cardboard tubes with metal bottoms. Tin cans make the best sound, but be careful of sharp edges. If you can collect enough posh coffee tins, then you're away!
- Hammer; nail; strong, heavy string; soapy water; cloth or sponge

Turn your can upside down and use the hammer and nail to punch a hole in the bottom, big enough to pass the string through. (You could punch the hole with a bradawl or a strong pin, but using a hammer and nail adds a nice constructional feel to the activity.)

Take about 30 cm of string, tie a knot in one end and thread it through the hole, leaving the knot on the inside of the can. Using a cloth or sponge, soak the string in the soapy water. Then, holding the can in one hand, pull your fingers along the string from the bottom of the can to the other end. The noise is wonderful.

Experiment with rubbing the string over and around a wax candle rather than dipping it in soapy water if you want to extend the activity. See how different types of can and different strings will change the noise that you make.

Talk about

- Do you like the noise you can hear?
- Does God like hearing our squawking noise?
- How else can we worship God?

Lego™ kart racing

Mess rating 2/5 • Danger rating 1/5 • Difficulty 1/5

I really like any kind of activity that encourages people to be individually creative. The Lego™ karts can be used whenever you have a Bible story that involves travelling (we used them for Epiphany and the magi travelling on their camels).

If you simply provide a ramp and a box of Lego™, people can create their own kart and see which design will work best.

Themes

Travelling (for example, Abraham, the magi or Mary and Joseph); **running the race**

Craft outline

You will need

- A big box of Lego™ (including several sets of Lego™ wheels)
- A ramp (we used a scaffold board taped securely to a stepladder)
- Pictures of camels and donkeys to cut out and colour in (optional)

Set up the ramp in advance. Make sure it's secure and is not going to get knocked over.

Empty out the Lego™ and set the challenge to build a kart (or set a cardboard donkey or camel on a Lego™ base with wheels). See whose kart travels the furthest when it's released from the top of the ramp.

Talk about

- Have you ever been on a mystery journey? How did it feel – exciting or scary?
- How must it feel to trust God and travel somewhere, even when you don't know what you might find on your journey?

Wooden boats

Mess rating 3/5 • Danger rating 5/5 • Difficulty 4/5

Making stuff out of wood is one of the things that we enjoy most at our Messy Church. It's a bit dangerous, especially if you allow everyone to have a go at hammering nails and sawing wood, but it's worth the effort and, provided it's well supervised, there is no reason why anything should go wrong.

These boats are very simple, and my niece still has hers in the bath two years after making it.

Themes

> **Noah** (Genesis 6—9); **Jesus calms a storm** (Luke 8:22–25); **the call of the first disciples** (Matthew 4:18–22); **the miraculous catch of fish** (John 21:1–6)

Craft outline

You will need

- Timber: for example, a length of 38 mm x 89 mm CLS (the stuff with rounded edges that builders use for studwork) and a 21 x 34 mm roofing batten
- Nails; wood glue; hammer; saw (a tenon saw is best)
- Gloves; goggles

These instructions are just a guide: if you have pieces of timber lying around, you may want to design a boat using what's available.

Cut out the base of the boat from your larger piece of wood. For example, use a tenon saw to cut a hull-shaped chunk of wood with 45° angles at each end. The side view will look something like this:

There is no reason why you can't cut out this shape during Messy Church, although you might choose to do it in advance to save time.

Use the smaller piece of wood to make the top half of the boat. This piece can easily be cut at Messy Church: sawing through a little piece of batten is quick and easy, even for the smallest child. However, you will need a sawing block resting on a table, and you will need to help carefully if children want to have a go. You may want to use gloves and goggles at this point.

A sawing block looks like the illustration below. You can buy them, but it's much cheaper and very easy to make your own. You hook one end of the block over the edge of the table and push the timber you are cutting firmly against the other end of the block.

To attach the top piece of wood to the bottom, dab it with a little wood glue and then nail it together with suitable wood nails.

There is no reason to exclude children from this part of the activity. Just be careful with the glue, and make sure that you hold the nail and guide the hammer, particularly when working with the smaller children. Parents will enjoy the risk that you take of having your fingers whacked with a hammer!

Once fixed, the top and bottom pieces of the boat will look like this:

To download the diagrams, go to **messychurch.org.uk/extremecrafts**

If you wish, you can paint your boats. Either use waterproof paint or point out that the boats are not suitable for floating.

Talk about

- Who does the building and DIY at your home?
- Can you imagine floating on your boat, out at sea or on a lake?
- What kinds of things would you do if you could sail away on your boat?
- How do you think the disciples felt when the storm blew up?
- What was going through Noah's mind as he built his boat miles away from any sea?'

Straw marble runs

Mess rating 3/5 • Danger rating 3/5 • Difficulty 3/5

A bit like making your own bagatelle board or pinball machine, this activity is bound to attract lots of interest and provides a great toy to take home at the end of Messy Church.

Themes

> **The wide and narrow paths** (Matthew 7:13–14); **journeys** (for example, the road to Emmaus or Abraham in the desert); **exploring; following Jesus**

Craft outline

You will need

* Lots of straws; cardboard cereal boxes; glue (ideally, a glue gun); paint or colouring pens; marbles

Cut each box in half along the narrow sides, to leave a board with a 2–3 cm lip around the edges. Using paint or pens, colour in the board.

Cut the straws into lots of different lengths, arrange them on the board in your desired pattern and glue them down. You need to design the runs so that if you prop up the top end of the board on a book or two and release a marble at the top, the marble will roll backwards and forwards across the board, making its way to the bottom.

Talk about

- Have you ever been on a journey?
- What's it like to follow someone?
- What's it like to follow Jesus?
- Why do you think God often doesn't make it very clear where we are going in our lives?

Smartphone projector

Mess rating 1/5 • Danger rating 1/5 • Difficulty 3/5

In this activity, the kids get to create their very own cinema – a pin-hole camera for the digital generation.

Themes

Faith (2 Corinthians 4:18; **5:7**); **seeing** (Mark 8:25); **God's knowledge of us** (Hebrews 4:13); **recognising Jesus** (Luke 24:31)

Craft outline

You will need

- Shoebox (or similar size box) with a tight-fitting lid
- Magnifying glass (without a handle)
- Black electrical tape or hot glue gun
- Pencil; play dough; craft knife
- Smartphone

A small plastic magnifying glass is fine, but the bigger the better, and a glass one with a detachable handle is best if you can get it. If you are using plastic, you should be able to saw off the handle.

On one of the short ends of the box, draw around the magnifying glass, then carefully cut out the circle to make a hole the same size as the glass. Wedge the glass into the hole and secure it with the tape or glue gun, making sure that it sits tightly and that no light can escape around the edges.

Put a large lump of play dough in the bottom of the box, towards the opposite end from the glass. Sit the phone securely on to the play dough, with the screen facing the magnifying glass. You will have to adjust the positioning of the phone, depending on the size of your magnifying glass.

Start playing a slideshow or film on the phone and close the box lid. Turn the lights down in the room and place your projector close to a wall. You can adjust the quality by moving the box closer to or further away from the wall, as well as by moving the phone backwards or forwards inside the box.

If you want to add sound, poke a hole in the back of the box with a pencil to stick a lead through from an external speaker.

Talk about

- How precious is our sight?
- God sees everything. Are there things we do that we wish God didn't see?
- Faith – knowing that God is with us even if we can't see him
- What do you think Jesus would look like today if he walked into the room?

Mini marshmallow crossbows

Mess rating 2/5 • Danger rating 4/5 • Difficulty 3/5

Weapons in church… really? Crossbows don't appear in the Bible, but bows and arrows do. This is a good craft for one of the older congregation members to run. It can be used if you are talking about battles in the Bible or in a talk about the good Samaritan: you can act out the story, with bandits attacking the man and firing marshmallows at him.

Themes

> **Biblical battles; the good Samaritan** (Luke 10:30–37); **Joshua and the battle of Jericho** (Joshua 6:1–21)

Craft outline

You will need

- Various lengths of wood around 3 cm x 6 cm in cross-section, which the children will cut down to 10 cm long
- Hammer; nails (not too thin); saw; sandpaper; elastic or elastic bands

Supervise children as they cut a 10 cm length of wood and sand all the edges smooth. You then need to hammer in two nails along one of the 6 cm sides so that they stick out to about 1 cm. Put an elastic band around the two nails or tie some elastic between them. Place a mini marshmallow on the wood between the nails, pull it back in the elastic band and *fire*!

Talk about

- Biblical battles
- The story of the good Samaritan
- Why do we have wars?

Inner tube pencil case

Mess rating 3/5 • Danger rating 3/5 • Difficulty 3/5

This is a great way of recycling to end up with a really cool pencil case or pouch. Don't go and buy new inner tubes for this. I've found that if you ask your local bike shop nicely, they'll be only too happy to save up old tubes that they were going to throw away at the end of the week. A local bike shop close to us had around 50 each week to throw away! Old tubes full of patches make the best-looking cases.

Themes

Looking after the planet; creation; transformation, born again

Craft outline

You will need

- Old bike inner tubes
- Scissors
- Rotary cutter and cutting mat (optional)
- Leather hole punch
- Paper clips
- Paint pen marker or similar
- Darning needle

- Sticky Velcro (optional)
- Wet cloth and paper towel

To make a pencil case, start by cutting a section of tube around 35 cm long, then cut up the seam so you can open it out. It will be full of talcum powder, so be careful not to breath it; wipe it off with a wet cloth and paper towel to dry it.

Fold up 15 cm and then use the paper clips either side to hold it together. With the pen, mark some dots every 1 cm up each of the sides, not the flap. Now carefully use the hole punch to make a hole on each of the dots you have drawn so it goes through both layers of the tube on the left and the right.

With another piece of inner tube, cut two lengths around 30 cm long and about 5 mm wide. The rotary cutter would be great at this, but scissors are just as good. These thin strips will be used to sew the pouch up. Thread one of the thin rubber strips through the darning needle and through the bottom two holes on one side and tie a knot. Keep stitching up the side till you get to the top and tie off with another knot and trim the end bit. Repeat with the other side.

For the flap, you can use the scissors to round it off or whatever design you want to do. Fold it over and use the sticky Velcro to close or any other type of fixing you decide upon. If you are using sticky Velcro, though, make sure the sides are really clean with no powder residue.

Talk about

- Can you ride a bike?
- Have you ever fixed or help fix a puncture?
- Do you recycle at home, school or church?

Lego™ maze

Mess rating 2/5 • Danger rating 1/5 • Difficulty 2/5

With this activity, you can make small mazes or a giant one, up to you. Maybe even build some trap and obstacles as well.

Themes

> **Journeys; directions; losing our way; come to me** (Matthew 11:28)

Craft outline

You will need

- Lego™ and Lego™ boards
- Marbles

Using the big square Lego™ bases is best for this, but if you don't have any you can use all your flat pieces together to build a large flat board. Use the thin Lego™ single pieces to make an outer edge wall and then create thin maze walls with channels wide enough for the size of marble you are using. You'll probably find the Lego™ masters in your group creating some awesome elaborate maze creations.

Talk about

- Have you ever been on a journey?
- What can you use to help you go in the right direction?
- How can you know by following someone that they are going in the right direction?
- Is it hard to always stay on the right path?
- What's it like to follow Jesus?

Bird feeder

Mess rating 3/5 • Danger rating 4/5 • Difficulty 3/5

This is a really nice activity for all ages and a great take-home craft. You'll need to be careful with the drill, but it's a great way to teach children about tool safety.

Themes

> **God feeds the birds** (Matthew 6:26); **the fifth day** (Genesis 1:20); **soar on wings like eagles** (Isaiah 40:31); **I know every bird in the mountains** (Psalm 50:11)

Craft outline

You will need

- Plastic drink bottles (500ml work great but you can go bigger)
- Wooden dowels about 20cm long (you could also use pencils or wooden spoons)
- String
- Drill
- Hot glue gun (optional)
- Birdseed

Carefully drill a hole the same size as your wooden dowel, pencil or spoon halfway down the bottle from one side to the other. Rotate the bottle 90 degrees and repeat, but this time closer to the bottom. Now push your dowels through the holes so you have a cross shape with the wood sticking out both ends. If the wood is loose, you can use the hot glue gun to help keep them in.

Now drill a hole about 5 cm above each dowel. This is where the seeds will come out from. Drill a small hole through the top of the bottle lid and poke the string through. Tie a few knots in the string so it won't slip back through the hole in the lid. You can use the glue gun around the knot for extra security. You can use this string to hang them up. Finally, fill the bottles up with the birdseed.

Talk about

- What is your favourite bird?
- Would you like to be able to fly? Where would you go?
- Why should we care for animals?

Snow globe

Mess rating 4/5 • Danger rating 4/5 • Difficulty 4/5

This activity needs a bit of planning, but it's so worth it. You need someone who can take pictures of the participants, print them out and laminate them. These personalised snow globes make great presents for grandparents or a special keepsake and memory at home. Remember for safeguarding to delete all pictures taken of children, unless you have written permission.

Themes

> **The rain and snow come down from the heavens** (Isaiah 55:10); **Jesus calms the storm** (Matthew 8:23–28); **family; gifts; joy**

Craft outline

You will need

- Glass jars with screw-on lids
- Hot glue gun
- Small pebbles
- Laminator
- Printer
- Digital camera

- Scissors
- Sandpaper
- Water
- Baby oil
- Glitter (the larger type, not the fine stuff)

Take full length pictures of individual participants and then print them out so they are the right size to fit into the jar. A tech-savvy teen would be good to have on team who can do this. Then cut out the person from the background and laminate them in batches. Cut around the cut-out pictures again, making sure you have a border of the laminate all around the picture so they are waterproof.

Using the sandpaper, scratch up the inside of the jar lid. This will help the glue to stick better. Now hot glue the bottom of the picture to the inside of the lid, taking care that it stands up nice and straight. Hot glue some pebbles to the lid around the picture, which will help it stand up as well. Take care not to go too close to the edge so that the lid can still screw on to the jar.

Now fill the jar with water almost to the top, add three teaspoons of baby oil and chuck in a bunch of glitter. Carefully replace the lid on to the jar being careful with the edges of the picture and screw it tightly shut. Give it a shake and you've got you own personal snow globe.

Talk about

- Do you like playing in the snow?
- Gifts, giving and receiving
- Joy in the small things
- Storms in our lives

Drinks carton boats

Mess rating 2/5 • **Danger rating 2/5** • **Difficulty 2/5**

Jesus did so much on or around boats. If you have a small paddling pool, it will add to the experience and can also be used during the celebration.

Themes

Noah (Genesis 6–9); **Jesus calms a storm** (Luke 8:22–25); **the call of the first disciples** (Matthew 4:18–22); **the miraculous catch of fish** (John 21:1–6)

Craft outline

You will need

- 1-litre juice or milk carton
- Scissors
- Acrylic paints
- Paper drinking straws
- Thick patterned paper or card
- Tape or glue
- Plasticine

Make sure the drinks cartons are washed clean and dry inside. Cut around and remove the pouring spout, then cover the hole by gluing some card over it. Lie the carton down on its side so the lip at the top of the carton is vertical, not horizontal. Carefully cut out a rectangle on the side of the carton that is facing up.

Paint your boat. If you have time, two coats are better to cover any of the existing packaging.

Cut a triangle of the patterned paper and stick it to the paper straw to make the sail, checking the height of the straw as you may need to make the sail shorter. Squash a ball of plasticine to the bottom of the boat inside the carton and stick the straw sail into the ball making sure it's standing up straight. You can now add toy figures if you have them to the boats and sail them in the paddling pool.

Talk about

- Have you ever been on a boat?
- How do you think the disciples felt when the storm blew up?
- Where would you like to sail on your boat?
- Some people find being by water peaceful. Where do you find your place of peace?

Noughts and crosses

Mess rating 3/5 • Danger rating 1/5 • Difficulty 3/5

This is an old game that's so quick to learn, fun for all ages and a great way to while away some time together. Creating your own set rather than drawing on paper also makes it more of an event.

Themes

> **Following the rules** (2 Timothy 2:5); **winning the race** (1 Corinthians 9:24–26); **spending time with others**

Craft outline

You will need

- Paper straws
- Card
- Pebbles (ten per person or family group)
- Glue
- Paint

Cut the card into 15 cm square pieces, one per person. Stick the straws around the edge of the card and then use them to create a 3x3 grid, cutting them down where necessary. Decorate the card and straws with the paint or anything else you might have. Take ten pebbles and paint five of them one colour and the other five another. These are your playing pieces.

Talk about

- Do you like to play games?
- Do you think Jesus might have played games with the disciples?
- Is it important to always win?
- How do you feel if someone doesn't want to play with you?

Balancing nails

Mess rating 3/5 • Danger rating 2/5 • Difficulty 5/5

Not really a craft at all but a great puzzle for all ages. Even when you know how it is done, it's still a challenge to complete. Young and old working together coming up with ideas for solutions is great to watch.

Themes

Waiting and patience (Romans 8:25); **not giving up** (Galatians 6:9); **anger** (Ecclesiastes 7:9); **perseverance** (Romans 5:4)

Craft outline

You will need

- Small block of wood (one per activity)
- 12 x 6-inch large flat head nails (per activity)
- Hammer

Start before the session by hammering one of the nails into the middle of each of the blocks so they can stand up. Make sure the nail is nice and straight. You could always pre-drill a hole to help with this. At the session give each group a block with nail in it as well as eleven more nails. The challenge is to try and balance all eleven nails on top of the nail in the block.

Here is a YouTube video with the solution: **youtu.be/9xtXg_6C8QE**

Talk about

- Did you think it was impossible at the start?
- Did you want to give up at any point? Why or why not?
- Learning from our mistakes

Gone fishing game

Mess rating 2/5 • Danger rating 1/5 • Difficulty 2/5

This is a great game that you have to build first. Children will love competing against the adults, and you can turn it into a big competition with stopwatches and scoreboards.

Themes

The parable of the net (Matthew 13:47–50); **patience; discovering Jesus; any Bible verse you choose**

Craft outline

You will need

- Empty plastic drink bottles
- Coloured card
- Scissors
- Glue
- Pens and pencils
- Sequins, rice, confetti, tissue paper
- Paint

Beforehand, write out some Bible verses on to the coloured card and then cut out the individual words, keeping them groups of individual verses, one per activity. Cut up the tissue paper into small squares. You can keep the rice as it is or beforehand mix it with some paint and then let it dry to make coloured rice.

Each person takes an empty bottle and fills it up about a quarter full of rice, tissue paper squares, sequins, confetti and the cut-up Bible verse and screw the lid on. Now draw and decorate fins and a tail on to the card and cut them out. Glue these to the bottle. Draw some eyes as well or use googly eyes if you have them and add these to the bottle as well. Now all you have to do is shake the bottle to mix it all up and then see how quickly you can find the words in the Bible verse in order rotating the bottle.

Talk about

- What was your favourite part of this activity – building or playing?
- We are all searching for something
- Praying and waiting

Newspaper bridges

Mess rating 2/5 • Danger rating 1/5 • Difficulty 4/5

This activity is great for working in teams. In fact, I've borrowed it from a team-building exercise I did. You can do boys vs girls, children vs adults, a bit of friendly competition is great. You can put a bit more pressure on with a ten-minute time limit.

Themes

Jesus helps with our burdens (Matthew 11:28–30); **helping others** (Galatians 6:2); **working with Jesus** (Philippians 4:13)

Craft outline

You will need

- Newspapers
- Tape
- Scissors
- Chairs
- Bibles
- Stopwatch

Give each team two or three newspapers, a roll of tape and a few pairs of scissors. Each team will also need two chairs facing each other with the closest edges about 50cm apart. Each team then has to try and make a bridge from one chair to the other with just the newspaper and tape alone. You can use a stopwatch to time them ten minutes if you want. Once they have built their bridge, it needs to be able to hold the weight of a Bible. You can award points for style, ingenuity or even how many Bibles they can hold.

Talk about

- Did you enjoy working in a team?
- Did you find it hard listening to other people's ideas if they were different to yours?
- Did your bridge carry more weight than you thought it would?
- Did the time limit put pressure on you and make it harder?

Newspaper towers

Mess rating 2/5 • Danger rating 1/5 • Difficulty 4/5

This activity is similar to the newspaper bridges in that you can turn it into a team competition and add a time limit. Instead of bridges, though, here you need to build the tallest self-supported tower. This is great to get people working together and sharing ideas.

Themes

> **The tower of Babel** (Genesis 11:1–9); **the wise and foolish builders** (Matthew 7:24–27); **the cost of being a disciple** (Luke 14:28–30); **encouraging and building others up** (1 Thessalonians 5:11)

Craft outline

You will need

- Newspaper
- Tape
- Scissors
- Stopwatch
- Measuring tape

Give each team three newspapers, a roll of tape and a few pairs of scissors. If you're timing the teams, give them ten minutes to try to build the tallest tower that is self-supported only using the paper and tape. The tallest tower wins, which needs to stand on its own for a count of ten. Award points for design and teamwork.

Talk about

- How we can grow stronger in our faith
- How we can help God build his church
- Did you have fun working in a team?
- How could you of made your tower better or stronger?

Science crafts

Oobleck

Mess rating 5/5 • Danger rating 1/5 • Difficulty 2/5

This is a great craft for the science geeks – a non-Newtonian fluid or 'Oobleck'. When we made this at our Messy Church, everyone said they would be trying it again at home. It's a fluid that, when struck or grabbed, goes hard and, when released, turns back to a fluid.

Themes

> **Creation of dry land** (Genesis 1:9); **the parting of the Red Sea** (Exodus 14:21); **walking on water** (Matthew 14:22–33); **living water** (John 7:37–39); **trust; faith**

Craft outline

You will need

- Five boxes of cornflour; water; food colouring (optional)
- Washing-up bowl; wooden spoon
- Clingfilm; thin metal tray
- Speaker or subwoofer and sound system able to play strong bass (optional)

In the washing-up bowl, add water and food colouring to a boxful of cornflour. Stir, adding more cornflour and water until you have used up all five boxes of flour. After a while, it will get quite tough to mix, but keep going – stirring slowly or using your hands. You'll know when you're finished because you'll be able to pour the mixture but, if you hit it, it will become solid.

For added fun, lay the speaker on its side and cover it well with clingfilm to protect it. Place the metal tray on top. Pour some of the Oobleck on to the tray and turn on the music. Make sure you hold the tray down so that the sound vibrates through. You may need to try different music to get the right effect, and a low frequency is best. When it's set up correctly, watch your Oobleck come alive and dance.

If you want to take it even further and your budget will stretch, make enough Oobleck to fill a small paddling pool. Take your shoes and socks off and walk across it. Yes, that's right, you can actually walk on it – but don't stop, or you'll sink. Search YouTube to find videos of people walking across a swimming pool of the stuff.

Talk about

- How do you think the disciples felt when they saw Jesus walking on water?
- How do you think Peter felt when he walked on water towards Jesus?
- God can do anything
- On the third day, God said, 'I command the water under the sky to come together in one place, so there will be dry ground' (Genesis 1:9, CEV)
- How can we have 'living water' (John 7:38)? What did Jesus mean by this?

Lava lamps

Mess rating 2/5 • Danger rating 2/5 • Difficulty 1/5

We're going old-school retro, back to the 1970s with good old lava lamps (disco music optional).

Themes

Separation of the waters (Genesis 1:6–7); story of Jonah;
Jesus calming the storm (Luke 8:22–25); lamp on a lampstand
(Luke 8:16)

Craft outline

You will need

- Small empty water bottles with tops
- Food colouring; water; cheap vegetable oil
- Fizzy tablets (such as Alka-Seltzer™)

Fill a small water bottle three-quarters full of vegetable oil and top up with water. The oil and water will separate, with the water at the bottom. Now add a few drops of food colouring to the bottle. It will fall through the oil and change the colour of the water. Add enough to make the water a bright colour.

Break a fizzy tablet in half, drop it into the bottle and screw on the lid. The tablet will fall through the oil and start fizzing in the water, creating coloured bubbles that shoot up through the oil. When it stops fizzing, add the rest of the tablet.

To take the craft one step further, make a base that can hold a torch to light up the lamp for full retro coolness, or add some glitter.

Talk about

- The universe
- How big and unexplored the oceans are
- Jesus, the light of the world

CD hovercrafts

Mess rating 2/5 • Danger rating 4/5 (use glue gun or superglue) • Difficulty 2/5

These hovercrafts are supercool and offer loads of opportunity for experimenting to find the best way to make them work.

Themes

The Holy Spirit; Elijah and the rushing wind (1 Kings 19:11)

Craft outline

You will need

- Unwanted CDs, CD-ROMs or DVDs (available very cheap online, if necessary)
- Sports caps from water bottles; glue gun or superglue; balloons
- Electrical tape (optional); pins (optional); sharp knife (optional)

In advance, you may want to use a sharp knife to remove the burrs from the bottom of the sports cap, to make sure it sits securely on the CD.

Carefully squeeze glue around the bottom of the cap and then stick it on the centre of the CD. The use of a glue gun is preferable, as the glue will set almost instantly, although you will obviously have to be very careful that children don't get burnt.

With the sports cap closed, carefully inflate a balloon and, pinching it at the bottom of the neck to stop the air escaping, stretch it over the nozzle of the lid. Once it's in place, pull the sports cap open and watch your hovercraft lift up in the air and float around the tabletop.

If you want to take the experiment further, use different-sized balloons or stick some electrical tape over the hole in the CD and pierce little holes in it, to see if you can get it to hover well and last as long as possible.

Talk about

- Did you expect your CD to fly?
- How do you think these hovercrafts work?
- Why do you think the Holy Spirit is sometimes called a breath or a wind?

Coke and Mentos

Mess rating 5/5 • Danger rating 1/5 • Difficulty 2/5

This is a famous science experiment and lots of fun, with no end of applications and variations. When dropped into a bottle of Coke, Mentos cause thousands of bubbles to form incredibly quickly. The Coke fizzes ferociously and sprays out of the neck of the bottle. The spray can reach several metres in the air, and, for this reason, it's definitely an outdoor activity.

The experiment does work with other mints and other fizzy drinks. We usually use the cheapest cola we can find, but tend to stick with branded Mentos.

Themes

The Holy Spirit; joy; evangelism; blessings

Craft outline

You will need

- Bottles of cola
- Mentos

This is a really simple activity but you can adapt it as you see fit. At its most basic, you need to open a brand-new bottle of cola, dump as many Mentos through the opening as you can and then run away. Try to set the bottle up so that it won't fall over.

Feel free to experiment with systems of getting more Mentos into the bottle. You can try using paper cones or more ingenious methods of your own devising. You can also incorporate an element of competition, seeing who can get the highest spray from their bottle.

Talk about

- Do you ever have something inside that's so exciting, you think you'll burst if you don't tell someone?
- How does it feel to tell someone some really good news?
- Why do you think Christians want to tell people about what they believe?

Sauce sachet diver

Mess rating 1/5 • Danger rating 1/5 • Difficulty 1/5

This is a really simple but clever science trick. Either make a sachet diver as a demonstration or, even better, have enough equipment available for everyone to make one.

Themes

Sadness and happiness; Peter greeting Jesus on the beach (John 21:7); **Peter walking on water** (Matthew 14:22–33)

Craft outline

You will need

- Empty drinks bottles (1 litre preferably, or 500 ml)
- Water
- Unopened sauce sachets

In advance, check that your sauce sachets float, as the experiment will only work with floating sachets. Check it again on the day, because different atmospheric pressures can change the effectiveness of the experiment.

Carefully push the unopened sauce sachet into the bottle and fill the bottle right to the brim with water. Once it's completely full, screw the lid on tight.

The sachet should float at the top of the bottle, but, if you then squeeze the bottle, the sachet will drop to the bottom.

This looks like a cool magic trick but is actually a well-known scientific experiment called a cartesian diver. As you compress the bottle, the small amount of air in the sauce sachet gets compressed until it is no longer able to keep the sachet buoyant. When you let go of the bottle, the air expands once more and the sachet floats back to the top.

Talk about

- What makes you feel happy? What makes you feel sad?
- How does it feel to know that God is with us no matter how we feel?
- Why did Peter want to walk on water? Why did he sink?
- Do you think you would be brave enough to step out of a boat and walk to Jesus on the water?

Ice balls

Mess rating 4/5 • Danger rating 2/5 • Difficulty 3/5

This is not really a craft; it's more like a game to play in the summer months if you are able to take some of your Messy Church sessions outside.

Themes

Competition (1 Corinthians 9:25); **winning** (1 Corinthians 9:24–27; 2 Timothy 2:5; 1 John 5:4)**; losing** (Mark 8:34–38); **perseverance** (Philippians 3:12–14); **sportsmanship** (Philippians 2:3)

Craft outline

You will need

- Water balloons
- Food colouring
- Freezer
- Chalk

Add a few drops of food colouring to a water balloon, fill with water and tie a knot in the end. Put your balloons in a freezer for a couple of days until they are nice and solid. (If you have the space, hang them up, to keep them as round as possible.) Then cut off the balloon knot, leaving a frozen coloured ball.

Use the chalk to mark out a target outside the church on a car park (if it's safe) or patio area. Take turns to throw or slide the ball to see who can get closest to the middle of the target.

Talk about

- Have you ever watched the Winter Olympics?
- Competition
- Winning and losing
- Perseverance
- Sportsmanship

Invisible writing

Mess rating 2/5 • Danger rating 3/5 • Difficulty 1/5

Here's another cool chemistry experiment, this time courtesy of the greengrocer. The technical name for it is 'steganography', the art of concealing a message within another message. It sounds like the stuff of James Bond, but the art of hiding messages can be traced back to 440BC and the ancient Greeks.

Themes

Holy Spirit; God speaking to us; prayer

Craft outline

You will need

- Lemons or a bottle of pure lemon juice; water
- Paper; pencils; cotton buds; lamp or candle
- Salt and wax crayon (optional)

Use the pencil to write or draw a fake message on the paper.

Add a few drops of water to a small cup of lemon juice. Dip a cotton bud into the water and lemon, write your real message or draw a picture on the paper and leave the paper to dry. When you want to reveal the message, hold the paper up to the candle (be very careful) or lamp (safer).

This experiment works because lemon juice is acidic and weakens the paper. Even when the paper is dry, the acid remains. When put near a heat source, the acid-covered parts burn and turn brown before the rest of the paper does.

Another way to reveal your message is to sprinkle salt over the drying lemon juice. After a minute, when the juice is dry, wipe the salt off and colour over the paper with the wax crayon.

Talk about

- Jesus appearing to the disciples
- What might God want to reveal to you?

Fossil prints

Mess rating 4/5 • Danger rating 1/5 • Difficulty 3/5

We know dinosaurs existed – we have fossils and bones to prove it – but when? How long ago? Before human beings or with them? There are so many questions that we can't really answer. Some people say there were dinosaurs on the ark, maybe as babies or even as eggs. Scientists lay out their evidence, but we don't really know, so let's just agree that they're cool and give people an opportunity to share their thoughts.

Themes

Creation; Behemoth and Leviathan (Job 40:15—41:34)

Craft outline

You will need

- 8 tbsp flour
- 8 tbsp used coffee grounds from a cafetière or coffee machine
- 4 tbsp salt
- 4 tbsp sand
- Water; card; seashells

The quantities listed above are per person. You can make a big batch and divide it up, but it's more fun to get the children to measure out their own quantities.

Mix the flour, coffee, salt and sand together. Add the water a little at a time until you get a thick dough, not too wet or too crumbly.

Flatten the dough out on to a piece of card, to a thickness of a couple of centimetres. Take your shells and press them into the mixture. Carefully remove them, leaving a 'fossil print' behind.

The prints can take a couple of days to dry out fully, so they will need to be left on the cards if you want to transport them.

Talk about

- God creating the world
- Things that scare us
- God's protection

Protect the egg

Mess rating 1–5/5 • Danger rating 2/5 • Difficulty 4/5

If you drop a fresh egg from ten feet up, it can only end up one way – messy! It is called Messy Church, I guess, but your mission is to protect that little egg on its journey to the ground. Everyone will have an idea for how to do it, from complex engineering solutions to just covering it in bubble wrap.

Themes

Easter; trust; protection; faith

Craft outline

You will need

- Fresh eggs
- Polystyrene cups; eggboxes; bubble wrap; newspaper; elastic bands; string; straws; any oddments of junk that look useful

Work in groups or individually to use the materials to protect the egg from smashing when it is dropped. Ask an adult to stand on a chair or a stepladder to drop the eggs safely.

Talk about

- Easter (eggs and new life)
- Is it easy to believe and trust that God will protect us?

Exploding lollipop sticks

Mess rating 1/5 · Danger rating 1/5 · Difficulty 5/5

This is a complicated activity that is difficult to explain and will need to be practised, but the result is visually exciting and well worth the effort.

Themes

> **Consequences of sin; 'Pay it forward'** (generous acts); **evangelism; mission**

Craft outline

You will need

- Tongue depressors (available online) or lollipop sticks (if you have them to hand); floor space

By weaving together lollipop sticks in a certain fashion, and holding them under tension, you can create a long chain reaction. If you build carefully, you can eventually release the end lollipop stick and a chain reaction of mini 'explosions' will occur, firing the sticks in the air. If you think it's not worth the effort, search YouTube for 'stick bombs' to see what you can create.

It's worth noting that this activity really does require practice before Messy Church and that smaller children are unlikely to be able to do it by themselves, but dads and older boys will become obsessed.

The sticks need to be woven together in a repeating pattern, as shown below.

To download the diagram, go to **messychurch.org.uk/extremecrafts**

Talk about

- What's your favourite story about Jesus? Who could you pass it on to?
- How does it make people feel when we are generous or kind to them?
- Why do you think it's good to say 'sorry' straight away when we have done something wrong?

Prayer flowers

Mess rating 1/5 • Danger rating 0/5 • Difficulty 2/5

This craft may not seem very extreme, but it's really cool and it involves science. I took the idea to a village called Namalemba in Uganda, where I did Messy Church at the Sunday school, and it was an experience I will never forget. The children were captivated by it. After the flowers had opened, they carefully took them out of the water and dried them in the sun to keep.

Themes

Prayer; creation

Craft outline

You will need

- Coloured paper; scissors; a cup or beaker; coloured pencils and crayons
- Bowls of water, or saucers and tablespoons

Draw round the cup or beaker to make a circle on a piece of paper. Then draw six or seven petals around the outside of the circle and cut out your flower shape.

Write a prayer inside the circle, and colour it. Fold the petals over so that they cover the prayer. They will overlap, leaving you with a roughly shaped circle.

Drop the flower gently into the bowl of water or add a tablespoon of water to the saucer and place the flower on top. Think about the prayer you wrote.

Here comes the scientific bit. When the paper touches the water, it will start to open by something called capillary action. The paper absorbs the water very quickly and, when paper gets wet, it swells, which causes the petals to open up.

Talk about

- Praying and waiting
- New life
- The amazing wonders around us

Exploding art

Mess rating 5/5 • Danger rating 2/5 • Difficulty 2/5

This is a combination of various activities that are written about on the internet. It mixes explosion, paint and mess to create amazing works of art.

Themes

Joy; creation; being filled with the Spirit

Craft outline

You will need

- Huge sheets of paper
- Either: film canisters; slightly watered-down tempura paint; fizzy tablets (similar to Alka Seltzer™)
- Or: vinegar; food colouring; small ziplock bags

Place the ingredients in a container, seal as quickly as possible, place on the paper, then step back and watch the explosion.

Talk about

- What pictures can you see in the explosion art?
- Do you ever feel excitement building up inside like this, feeling as if you're going to pop?
- What do you think God might want to do with your passions?

Mobius strips

Mess rating 0/5 • Danger rating 0/5 • Difficulty 2/5

This is a mind-bending physics/maths trick, where participants get to make an impossible shape.

Themes

Infinity; God; space; love

Craft outline

You will need

* Sheets of A4 paper; scissors; pens; glue or double-sided tape

This is an unbelievably simple activity with astonishing results. Cut a strip from your sheet of A4 paper, 3 or 4 cm in width. Twist one end of the strip at 180° and attach it to the other end with the glue or tape. Run your finger along the strip to discover that it has only one surface – which should be impossible!

To make it more complicated, write the words 'ever and ever and ever and' along the strip of paper so that it looks as if the words never end. You can do this either once the loop is completed or, to make it even more difficult, before you glue the ends together (much harder than you'd think).

Once you've made your loop, try cutting the strip in half lengthways (the dotted line in the diagram below) to make another, double-sized, loop with four twists. Cut that in half too and you'll end up with two Mobius strips looped inside each other.

Finally, try making a giant strip using newspaper or other huge sheets of paper.

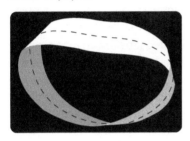

To download the diagram, go to **messychurch.org.uk/extremecrafts**

Talk about

- How does it make you feel when you think about the size of the universe? What's it like to be friends with a God who is that big?
- Can you imagine spending eternity with God?
- Psalm 103:12 says that our sins are taken as far from us as the west is from the east. What do you think that means?

Big bottle rocket

Mess rating 4/5 • Danger rating 4/5 • Difficulty 3/5

This is an activity to really get the dads involved and have a competition to see who can go the highest. When we did this at our Messy Church, one of our leaders Adrian tested it before anyone came, to see if it would work. I had my doubts… it worked… we got wet… it was awesome!

Themes

Being filled with the Spirit; joy; ascension; evangelism

Craft outline

You will need

- Plastic 2-litre drink bottle
- A cork
- Bike pump with flexible hose and a needle adaptor
- Water
- Card for fins and nose cone (optional)

Push the needle adaptor through the cork. It has to go all the way through, so if your cork is too long just trim the cork down. Add a cone to the bottom of the bottle (this will become the top) and add some fins as well.

Fill the bottle a quarter full of water and push the cork in tightly. Take it outside (IMPORTANT) and connect the pump to the needle adaptor. If your fins are strong enough, it should stand up by itself. We ended up digging a little hole for it to sit in, so it stayed upright. Make sure everyone is standing back and start pumping air into the bottle. After a few seconds, the bottle will lift off fast and high with a trail of water.

Talk about

- Have you ever been so excited you feel like you might burst?
- The planets that God made that we are starting to explore
- God created the stars and knows them by name

Mini bottle rocket

Mess rating 4/5 • Danger rating 2/5 • Difficulty 2/5

This is the mini version of our bottle rocket activities, but don't let the size fool you. This is just as fun and can be done inside depending on the height of your ceiling. Line a few up and have highest launch competition, or angle them slightly and see whose goes the furthest. Maybe even make a target to try and hit.

Themes

Holy Spirit; joy; space; faith and trust; he counts the stars and knows them by name (Psalm 147:4)

Craft outline

You will need

- An old 35 mm film canister (white style ones are the best)
- Fizzing tablet like Alka-Seltzer (cheaper alternatives are fine)
- Paper
- Water

Make a little cone and fins out of the paper and stick these to the canister, making sure that the cone is not on the lid end. Break the tablet in half. Take off the canister lid and put a teaspoon (5 ml) of water into the canister. Do this next bit quickly: drop the half tablet into the canister, replace the lid tightly and put it on the ground, cap side down, and step back and wait. About ten seconds later you'll hear a POP and the canister will launch into the air!

If for some reason the canister doesn't fire, wait around 30 seconds before investigating. Usually it just means the lid isn't on properly and the gas has escaped.

Talk about

- You might think you are small, but the Holy Spirit makes you powerful
- The International Space Station (ISS). Different countries coming together
- The universe
- Going out and spreading the good news of Jesus

Rainbow rain

Mess rating 4/5 • Danger rating 1/5 • Difficulty 2/5

It doesn't matter how old you are, this one appeals to everyone and will always bring a smile and an ahhhhh, oooooh, coooool.

Themes

Creation (Genesis 1:6); **Noah** (Genesis 9:12–17); **raining down righteousness** (Isaiah 45:8); **water; baptism**

Craft outline

You will need

- Shaving cream
- Food colouring
- Clear glass bowl or vase
- Small bowls or containers
- Eye dropper or teaspoon
- Water

Add some water to the small bowls and add some drops of food colouring to each of them. The less water, the more concentrated the colour; however the more water, the more rain you will get. You want at least four different colours. Now fill the glass bowl or vase with water about 2/3 full. Spray a generous bunch of shaving cream on top of the water in the bowl or vase.

Once your cloud is ready, use the eye dropper or teaspoon to drop different colours of water on to the shaving cream cloud. Slowly the coloured water will make its way through the cloud and then come out like rain into the water below.

Talk about

- Have you ever been caught in the rain and got soaked?
- Do you like the rain?
- Have you been baptised or been to a baptism?
- What do we need water for?

Magic drawing

Mess rating 3/5 • Danger rating 1/5 • Difficulty 3/5

This activity is guaranteed to bring a smile to everyone. It's so simple to do, but the end result is really cool. You're only limited by your imagination. You don't need to be a great artist – any squiggle will work.

Themes

Creation; resurrection; miracles; being filled with the Spirit

Craft outline

You will need

- Whiteboard markers (alcohol based)
- Glass bowl
- Water

Start by drawing a simple picture on the inside of the bowl. A good one to start with might be a stick figure. Now slowly pour some water into the bowl up to the edge of the picture you've drawn. As the water touches the picture, it will start to go underneath and lift it from the bowl. As the water moves, so will your picture be floating on the top.

Talk about

- Do you always need to see something to believe it?
- What do you think it would have been like being among the people who witnessed Jesus bringing someone back to life?
- Jesus washing away our sins
- What is your favourite miracle that Jesus did?

Walking water

Mess rating 2/5 • Danger rating 1/5 • Difficulty 2/5

This is a simple enough activity with a cool end result as you mix different colours to create something new. The science bit is 'capillary action'. Have fun experimenting with more containers in a line and mixing new colours.

Themes

Creation (Genesis 1:6); **Noah** (Genesis 9:12–17); **water; evangelism; waiting and patience**

Craft outline

You will need

- Three glasses
- Food colouring
- Paper towels
- Water

Fill two of the glasses with water, then line the three glasses up next to each other, with the empty glass in the middle. Drop some food colouring into the glasses with water in, so you have two different colours – blue and yellow work really well.

Fold a paper towel in half lengthways and then half again. Place one end of the paper into the first colour glass and bend it over into the middle empty glass. Do the same with the other colour glass, bending another paper towel into the middle glass. Now watch and wait as the colours walk up the paper towels and meet in the middle. Slowly the coloured water will mix and drip down into the glass, creating a new colour.

Talk about

- Sharing the good news of Jesus
- Praying and waiting
- Why is it so hard to wait for things?
- Growing in faith

Smoke ring cannon

Mess rating 2/5 • **Danger rating 4/5** • **Difficulty 4/5**

This activity is so much fun. You can make a bunch of these and have smoke rings flying all over the place. Done right, the smoke ring can have enough power to knock over thin plastic cups or houses of cards. The science bit: the smoke rings are called a 'toroidal vortex'. Be careful with the naked flame and the incense stick.

Themes

The Holy Spirit and Pentecost; **Jesus calms a storm** (Luke 8:22–25); **God creating man** (Genesis 2:7); **David's song of praise** (2 Samuel 22:9)

Craft outline

You will need

- A 1-litre plastic bottle
- Scissors
- Tape
- Balloon
- Matches
- Incense stick

Remove the bottom third of the bottle with the scissors. Cut the neck off the balloon, keeping the main round part.

Stretch the balloon over the open bottom of the bottle so it's tight like a drum. Use the tape to secure the balloon to the sides of the bottle. Light the incense stick and hold the open neck of the bottle above it until the bottle is full of smoke. To make smoke rings, tap or flick the balloon skin. Depending on how hard you do it, it will give different results.

Talk about

- How do you think the people felt when the Holy Spirit arrived sounding like a roaring wind?
- What things you can think of that are powered by wind?
- Were you surprised by the power of the wind?
- What did it feel like to be hit by a smoke ring?

Solar oven

Mess rating 3/5 • Danger rating 3/5 • Difficulty 5/5

This activity could have gone in construction, science or edible. It's great fun but best on a nice, hot summer's day in England – unless you're running your Messy Church in Australia and California (not jealous at all).

Themes

Faith (John 6:35); **generosity** (Proverbs 11:25); **feeding the 5,000** (Luke 9:10–17); **joy** (Nehemiah 8:10)

Craft outline

You will need

- Cardboard boxes (takeaway pizza boxes are best)
- Black paper
- Aluminium foil and cling wrap
- Craft knife
- Glue
- Ruler
- Pen
- Black electrical tape
- Long skewer

Start by drawing a square on the top of the pizza box lid about an inch in from the edge. Carefully using the knife and a ruler for straight lines, cut around the lines except from the line along the hinge of the box. Fold this flap back.

Put some glue on the inside of the flap and then line it with the aluminium foil (shiny side up). Fold the foil around the edges to help keep it in place and make sure to keep the foil as smooth as possible. Now cover the hole you made with some cling film and stick the edges down with the black tape (do this from the inside of the box), making sure there are no gaps. Line the inside of the box with foil, gluing it in place on the sides and bottom as well as the inside edges of the lid where you stuck the cling film. Glue a square of black paper centred to the bottom of the box (this helps retain heat). Now use the wooden skewer and some tape to prop the foil lid up at about 90 degrees from the rest of the box and it's all ready.

S'mores are really good to try with this or maybe just see how quickly you can melt a piece of chocolate. Lift up the lid with the cling film on and place your food on a small square of foil as a tray on top of the black paper. Close the cling film lid, keeping the foil lid open at 90 degrees and pointed towards the sun… and wait…

Talk about

- Do you help cook at home?
- What's your favourite meal?
- Why do you think a lot of Jesus' stories and ministry included food?
- Why do you think Jesus spoke about himself and his word as bread?
- Giving food to local food banks

Arty crafts

3D pictures

Mess rating 2/5 • Danger rating 1/5 • Difficulty 3/5

Anything 3D is fascinating, and these homemade drawings are easy to do. Be prepared: your fridge is probably going to be plastered with these pictures within a week.

Themes

> **The rainbow** (Genesis 9:12–17); **Joseph's coat of many colours** (Genesis 37:3–4); **creation of light** (Genesis 1:3)

Craft outline

You will need

- Paper; pencil; black marker or thick felt-tip pen; coloured pencils

Start by using the pencil to trace the outline of your hand lightly on the piece of paper. Now use the black marker to draw lines horizontally across the paper. Draw straight lines outside the outline and lines curving upwards inside the outline. This will make the hand look as if it's standing out from the paper (see the illustration opposite).

With the coloured pencils, colour in between the lines, making sure not to have the same colour stripes next to each other.

To download the diagram, go to **messychurch.org.uk/extremecrafts**

Talk about

- Have you ever seen a rainbow? What colours did you see?
- Have you got a favourite item of clothing? Why do you like it so much?
- Have you ever seen the colours that light makes, through a glass of water?
- Have you ever had to forgive or be forgiven by your brother or sister?
- Can you remember your dreams? Did they tell a story?
- Why did God flood the world?

Friendship bracelets

Mess rating 0/5 • Danger rating 2/5 • Difficulty 4/5

If you've got boys like mine who are in the Scouts, they love playing with rope and tying knots. These bracelets are not bits of coloured plaited string with charms on them: they're Bear Grylls-style cobra knot survival bracelets. They look great and are made to be taken apart easily, reverting to six feet of cord that can be used for any purpose – replacing a shoelace, making a simple washing-line on a camping trip, or tying your little brother up. (*Don't* tie your little brother up!)

Themes

Friendship; rescue; adventure

Craft outline

You will need

- Paracord (six to seven feet of cord per bracelet)
- Scissors; candle or lighter; tape measure; buckles (optional)

You can buy paracord online at sites such as **thebushcraftstore. co.uk,** for about 7p per foot. Various colours are available, as well as military camouflage designs. This site also sells buckles for £1.95 for five, but there are other ways to tie the bracelets without buckles.

Instructions for tying paracord bracelets are complicated. Go to **instructables.com/id/Paracord-bracelet-with-a-side-release-buckle/?ALLSTEPS** or search on YouTube for 'cobra knot paracord bracelet instructions'.

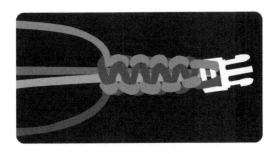

To download the diagram, go to **messychurch.org.uk/extremecrafts**

Talk about

- Have you ever had a problem that you weren't sure how to solve?
- Like a bracelet tied around our wrist, God is with us all the time
- Our journey with God through life can be like an adventure with ups and downs

Giant painting

Mess rating 5/5 • Danger rating 0/5 • Difficulty 2/5

This activity will fit with just about any theme you like and will make a perfect display for you to leave up after Messy Church.

Themes

Any theme – just decide on an appropriate picture and giant paint it.

Craft outline

You will need

- A huge papered floor area (ideally, outside); gallons of paint; massive paint brushes, rollers, and so on

Decide on a picture (or sketch one in advance) and then paint it as big as possible. The use of paint rollers and big exterior paintbrushes makes this an excellent activity for everyone.

Talk about

- Whatever the theme is for this Messy Church session

Soap carving

Mess rating 5/5 • Danger rating 3/5 • Difficulty 2/5

What child or dad doesn't like sitting down with a penknife and stick, whittling? This is the same thing, just a bit safer and easier.

Themes

Creation; washing our sins away; shaping our lives; prayer and reflection

Craft outline

You will need

- Bars of soap; dinner or butter knives (not too sharp)

Buy cheap packs of soap from pound shops. Try to get the sort with no square edges and no writing on them.

Take a bar of soap and a knife and just carve away. You are limited only by your own imagination. When we did this craft, we made crosses and fish and all kinds of funky designs. Some people prayed and then slowly carved a shape with their eyes closed. There are no hard and fast rules: just start carving and see what happens.

As the sculptor Michelangelo said, 'I saw the angel in the marble and carved until I set him free.'

Talk about

- Prayer
- Asking God to cleanse us and wash away our sins
- Jesus died on the cross, washing away our sins so that we can live with him in heaven
- God can smooth away our rough edges and shape us into the people he wants us to be
- Creative gifts such as sculpting

Shadow puppets

Mess rating 1/5 • Danger rating 2/5 • Difficulty 3/5

When we held a Messy Church service on the subject of 'fear', we decided to do lots of activities on a 'dark' theme. I had the idea of doing a shadow puppet show of the battle between David and Goliath, to think about turning shadows (often something scary) into something delightful (a way of retelling a story).

Whether it was because we were re-enacting a battle or whether the shadow theatre idea itself was popular, I don't know, but the boys loved the activity. They spent ages crafting their puppets, and then ages behind the screen, telling and retelling the story.

Themes

Light and darkness; fear

Craft outline

You will need

- Heavy card; split-pin fasteners; garden canes or similar sticks (30–40 cm long)

- A large rectangular frame, with a white sheet hanging over; table; chair
- A very bright light (such as a halogen spotlight)

Set up the theatre as in the diagram below.

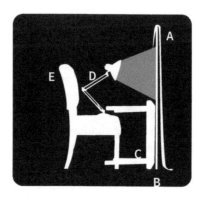

Key

A Sheet   **B** Frame
C Table on its side   **D** Lamp
E Chair

To download the diagram, go to **messychurch.org.uk/extremecrafts**

It's worth spending some time on the set-up to get it right. You need to be able to stand to one side of the chair but behind the lamp, operating your puppets between the lamp and the sheet, so that the only shadows visible are from the puppets rather than from your body. Take care with the spotlight, as it will get very hot.

To make the puppets, search on the internet for 'shadow puppet'. There are hundreds of different outlines available: you shouldn't have to make your own. The best templates come in several pieces so that your characters can be jointed to add movement. You can either make templates of the puppet shapes, and draw round and cut them out on the day, or you can pre-print several shapes for people to cut out.

Cut out each of the pieces, jointing them at the relevant places using the split-pin fasteners. Attach the garden canes to the back with sticky tape.

Experiment with the best place to attach the stick to each puppet. Let people work things out for themselves as much as possible, and give lots of space for problem-solving and creativity.

Talk about

- Are you afraid of the dark? Why/why not?
- How does it feel to be in the light?
- The Bible says, 'You belong to the light and live in the day. We don't live in the night or belong to the dark' (1 Thessalonians 5:5, CEV). What does this mean?

Origami boats

Mess rating 2/5 • Danger rating 1/5 • Difficulty 3/5

This is a nice craft for the older children and adults. There's something very satisfying about starting with a blank sheet of paper and ending up with a 3D model. But be warned: if you do this craft and have kids at home, your house will soon be overrun with paper boats. My two boys got the origami bug and it became hard to find a sheet of paper that hadn't been folded into some strange model.

Themes

> **Noah's ark** (Genesis 6—9); **Jesus walking on water** (Matthew 14:22–33); **'fishing for people'** (Matthew 4:19)

Craft outline

You will need

- A4 sheets of paper; coloured pencils and/or crayons
- Small paddling pool (supervised) with one or two inches of water
- Jelly babies or Lego™ figures (optional)

Make a few boats in advance to show what they should look like.

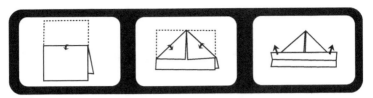

1 Fold an A4 piece of paper in half.

2 Fold the two top corners in to the centre. (You may need to make a crease first.)

3 Fold up the lower edge of the paper. Turn over and do the same on the other side.

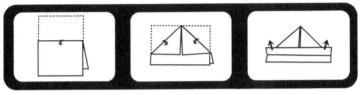

4 Tuck the corners of one of the rectangular sections in behind the triangle.

5 Hold the triangle near the top and squash it in, so that it collapses into a square shape.

6 Fold up the bottom corner of the square. Turn it over and do the same on the other side.

7 You should now have a shape that looks like this.

6 Holding the base and the top of the triangle, gently pull the points of the triangle apart and allow the sides to lift up. It should open up into a boat shape that will float on water.

To download the diagram, go to **messychurch.org.uk/extremecrafts**

Talk about

- How would it feel to be on a small boat at night, being tossed and turned in strong winds?
- Have you ever rowed a boat? Was it easy or hard?
- How do you think the disciples would have felt, seeing Jesus walking on the water towards them?
- Have you ever been fishing? Is it only enjoyable if you catch some fish?
- Jesus said that his disciples would 'fish for people'. Do you tell people about Jesus?
- Water can be fun but also, at times, scary
- How hard would it have been for Noah to build the ark by hand, with no power tools?

Wire and nail crosses

Mess rating 1/5 • Danger rating 2/5 • Difficulty 3/5

These crosses are inspired by some of the more manly Christian jewellery that was popular a while back, made out of heavy old-fashioned carpentry nails. Some bishops still wear crosses made in a similar fashion.

It's heavy, tough jewellery that's hard to make – extreme jewellery, you could call it.

Themes

Good Friday/Easter; grace; forgiveness; sacrifice

Craft outline

You will need

- Nails in two different sizes – some two-thirds the length of the others. You will need twice as many short nails as long. For example, to make 20 crosses you will need 20 x 15 cm nails and 40 x 10 cm nails
- Wire (thin enough to be bent and cut)
- Pliers (ideally, needle-nosed)
- Wire cutters

Nails can be expensive, so make time in advance to shop around.

Take two of the shorter nails and place them side-by-side, point to head. Using the pliers, wrap wire around the ends as tightly as you can, cutting off any excess and tucking the ends in neatly.

Take one long nail and place it across the two shorter nails to make a traditional cross shape. Carefully wrap more wire around the centre of your cross, as tightly as you can, to secure all three nails together.

Talk about

- What kinds of things do you use nails for?
- How do they feel in your hand?
- Why do you think that Jesus would allow himself to be killed on a cross?

Modelling balloon swords

Mess rating 2/5 • Danger rating 1/5 • Difficulty 2/5

Every bloke on the planet wishes he could have a go at modelling balloons – it's a well-researched fact!

There are many stories in the Bible that lend themselves to sword-making, yet we would normally shy away from anything like that at Messy Church. These 'swords' are so comical that they will probably take the edge off any fears about making weapons. That said, you may still get some parents who object, so be ready to make balloon dogs as well.

Themes

> **The sword of the Spirit and the armour of God** (Ephesians 6:11–17); **David and Goliath** (1 Samuel 17:22–54); **the garden of Gethsemane** (Mark 14:43–50)

Craft outline

You will need

- Modelling balloons: we recommend Qualatex 260Q (available online), as they are the easiest to inflate and model, and don't burst too easily.

- A balloon pump: this is absolutely vital, as modelling balloons are impossible to inflate without one.

Make sure you practise this craft in advance, and buy enough balloons to have a go at dogs, giraffes and hats at the same time. If you need help, search on the internet for 'modelling balloon sword'.

Carefully inflate the balloon, leaving an inch or two at the end uninflated. Knot the balloon (this is hard, and will need to be done by an adult).

Starting at the knotted end of the balloon, twist a small ball. Then, holding on to the ball, make another twist about 30 cm further up, and join that twist on to the ball twist.

Now take the other end of the balloon, pull it right back and feed it through the circle you have made with the first two twists. Pull the end right through until you have a handle and a good sword length.

Feel free to play around with the twists to make more intricate hand guards, and so on.

Dads will all want to have a go at modelling balloons and lots of the children will end up making more than one model, so have plenty of balloons available.

Talk about

- What kinds of people carry swords?
- Why do people in the Bible often fight battles, whereas we would usually want to be people of peace?
- Why does the Bible compare the word of God to a sword?

The amazing walk through a card trick

Mess rating 1/5 · Danger rating 0/5 · Difficulty 2/5

This is an old idea, but a good one. Set the challenge of cutting a hole in an index card that is big enough to step through.

Themes

Prayer; the armour of God (Ephesians 6:11–17); miracles

Craft outline

You will need

- Index cards; copies of the template below; scissors

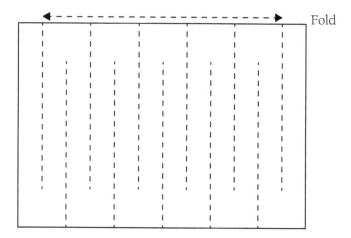

Fold

To download the diagram, go to **messychurch.org.uk/extremecrafts**

Fold the index card in half widthways before cutting slits in both sides, as shown by the broken lines in the template. Remember to cut a slit along the folded edge as well, as shown.

The more cuts you make in the sheet, the bigger your loop will be – but the thinner too, so be careful.

Open the final creation right out and step through. See how big a loop you can make. How many people can you encircle with one card?

Talk about

- Do you ever feel as if God has you surrounded by his love?
- Who else makes you feel like that?
- What things does God protect when he wraps us up in his love? What things does he keep out?

Crayon rain

Mess rating 5/5 • **Danger rating 4/5** • **Difficulty 3/5**

This is a great way to do a big piece of artwork that can then be put on display in church for all to see. You can do individual ones, but there will be increased mess, danger and cost. The end effect is really impressive and families will ask you to do it again for sure.

Themes

> **Creation day two** (Genesis 1:6–8); **joy; the rainbow** (Genesis 9:12–17); **washing our sins away**

Craft outline

You will need

- Lots of crayons
- Large canvas
- Hot glue gun
- Hairdryer(s)
- Black paper
- Scissors

Start by hot gluing the crayons to the top of the canvas so they are pointing down in a line. The effect works better if you have all the greens together and all the reds and pinks, etc. in their colour groups. Prop the canvas up at a slight angle with some scrap paper or sheeting on the floor. Now get the children and families to take it in turns with the hairdryer to start heating up the crayons. They will start to melt and run down the canvas, mixing the different colours and looking pretty awesome. It's nice to keep some of the bottom of the canvas white for contrast. You can also use the black paper to cut out small shapes of houses, schools, shops and the church to create your village and stick this in a line right at the bottom of the canvas.

Talk about

- Have you ever danced in the rain?
- Are you happy or sad when it rains?
- Water is life
- Praying for God's light and colour to soak our community

Messy flag

Mess rating 5/5 • **Danger rating 1/5** • **Difficulty 2/5**

A great activity for all ages and for all the Messy families and team to join in on. Plus you end up with a great way to let everyone know where you are.

Themes

Family; our names engraved on God's hands (Isaiah 49:16); identity

Craft outline

You will need

- A flat white single bed sheet
- Fabric paints or pens
- Paintbrushes or sponges
- Flag pole, long and strong bamboo cane or similar
- String or strong cord
- Sewing machine or a needle and thread (before session)

Start beforehand by taking the bed sheet and folding it in half. Sew around the edges. On one of the smaller edges, sew a pocket along the edge that you can slide the bamboo cane through, unless you decide to fix your flag to something you may already have existing.

Get everyone at your Messy Church, including team, to paint their hand with the fabric paint and make a hand print on the sheet. Use a pen to write their name and maybe even a prayer next to their hand. If you have a particularly arty person at your Messy Church, get them to paint a Messy logo. Read your paint instructions carefully. Most need to be ironed when dry to set the paint before washing.

Fly your flag with pride and let everyone know who you are and where you are.

Talk about

- Look at all the people who are part of your Messy Church, all different ages, genders, colours, but one family: God's children
- Do we let others know we are Christians? Why and how?
- Where else do you see flags?

Balloon painting

Mess rating 5/5 • Danger rating 4/5 • Difficulty 4/5

We have done this activity at a couple of Messy garden parties and it's gone down so well. We've even had a couple of passing police officers come in and have a go. The end result is a great piece of art to put up in church. This is best done outside unless you have spent a lot of time preparing the area. Paint goes further than you might think.

Themes

Creation; joy; beauty out of chaos; teamwork

Craft outline

You will need

- Large canvas
- Poster paint
- Balloons
- Balloon pump
- Two bamboo canes
- Drawing pin
- Tape
- String

Place the canvas flat on the floor. Carefully stick a drawing pin to the end of one of the bamboo canes. We did it by using a few strips of tape pierced by the pin and then taped to the cane. Attach a length of string about 1 m to the end of the other cane. Now take one of the balloons and blow it up and let it down a couple of times to get it a bit more supple. Squirt some paint into the balloon, then, using the balloon pump, carefully blow the balloon up. You can use your mouth but that can get really messy! Tie a knot in the balloon and then attach it to the string.

You're now ready to create some stunning art. Have one person hold the cane with the balloon hanging over the canvas then get another person to carefully use the other cane with the drawing pin attached to burst the balloon exploding paint all over the canvas. Keep going with other colours until you're happy with your messy work of art.

Talk about

- Do you think God had fun creating his masterpiece, the world?
- Sometimes when things don't go to our plan, they work out even better
- Working together can produce amazing results. Jesus worked with his disciples as a team

Glow sand pictures

Mess rating 5/5 • Danger rating 2/5 • Difficulty 2/5

We often do this activity at our Messy Light Party. It's so magical and always a favourite of all ages. You can get black lights from most hardware shops as well as Amazon. You can buy an actual light set or just bulbs. You will also need it quite dark to get the best effect, so you may have to use another room where you can close all the curtains.

Themes

I am the light of the world (John 8:12); let your light shine (Matthew 5:16); the Lord is my light, whom shall I fear? (Psalm 27:1)

Craft outline

You will need

- Epsom salt (you can find tubs of this in pound shops)
- Fluorescent paints
- Plastic ziplock bags
- A black light
- PVA glue and spreaders or brushes
- Card

Divide the Epsom salts in to various bags, depending on how many paints you are using. Squirt a bunch of paint in to each bag, close it and then massage it altogether to mix it thoroughly. Once mixed, open the bags to allow the air to dry the salt out. You could pour it out on to trays as a thin layer to dry quicker. A good 24 hours is needed for this. You may find it clumps together, but give it a quick mix and it will separate again. Put your coloured salt in to pots and it's ready to go.

For the activity, paint the glue on to the card and sprinkle the salt over the picture. Underneath the black light, these pieces of artwork will look amazing.

Talk about

- The salt only glows in the presence of the special light bulb. We too glow best in the presence of God
- How does the salt feel? Does it stick to your hands? Do they glow?
- What else glows under the special bulb?

Pendulum painting

Mess rating 5/5 • Danger rating 1/5 • Difficulty 3/5

This starts with a bit of construction and then ends with some amazing pieces of art reminding me of being a child and playing with my Spirograph set. You even get a bit of science and physics in this activity.

Themes

Creation; journeys; prayer

Craft outline

You will need

- Three broom stick handles or strong bamboo canes, each around 4 feet long
- String
- Large paperclips
- Empty 500 ml drink bottles with lids
- Poster paint and water
- Scissors
- Craft knife
- Lining paper
- Metal skewer or similar sharp, pointy thing

Begin by using some of the string to lash the three poles together at the top to make a tripod. Find a Scout to help you do it correctly, look on YouTube or just bodge it with string, tape, rubber bands, etc. As long as it's strong and stands up, it doesn't have to be pretty.

Take your 500 ml bottles and carefully cut the bottoms off of them. Using the skewer, make three or four evenly spaced-out holes around the edge of the bottle where you just removed the bottom. Tie a piece of string through each hole and then tie them all together in a knot so that the bottle hangs down straight. Tie these to a length of string with a paperclip at the opposite end. You will use the paperclip to easily hook to the string lashing the tripod together. The bottle wants to hang about one inch off of the floor, so adjust your string on each bottle. Unscrew the lid and, again using the skewer, poke a hole through the centre of the lid and then screw back on to the bottle.

Mix your paints with some water to a thin but not watery consistency. Place a piece of lining paper under the tripod. Half-fill a bottle with some paint, making sure to put your finger over the hole to stop the paint coming out. Now attach the string to the tripod with the paperclip. Hold the bottle to one side of the paper and let go! You'll create some really cool patterns. When you've finished, grab the bottle, remembering to cover the hole with your finger. Grab another colour and go crazy!

Talk about

- Is there a pattern to your life, good or bad?
- How easy is it to disrupt the pattern?
- What's the best journey you have been on?
- Can you pray for as long as it takes the pattern to be created?

String art

Mess rating 3/5 • Danger rating 4/5 • Difficulty 3/5

Another activity for children to learn how to use a tool, so safety is key here. The finished craft is great for putting on display at home. Again, like many of these activities, you could create a large one to display at church. If you go large, adding an LED light at the bottom, shining upwards, will light up the string and make a really striking display.

Themes

Doubting Thomas (John 20:25); **love and sacrifice of Jesus; abundance** (1 Chronicles 22:3); **encouraging others** (Isaiah 41:7)

Craft outline

You will need

- Wood (pallet wood is ideal)
- String
- 1-inch wire nails (flat head)
- Hammer
- Saw
- Pencil

- Paper
- Scissors
- Tape

Cut down the pallet wood to manageable lengths for each person. Draw an outline of a cross or heart or similar on the paper that will fit on the wood. Cut out the shape and then tape this to the wood. Carefully hammer the nails around the edge of the paper template, roughly one inch apart. Remove the template, leaving just the shape created by the nails.

Take the string and make a slip knot at one end. Place it over the head of one of the nails, pulling tight. Now wrap the string around the other nails to form the outline of your shape and then go in and out, up and down, creating an inner pattern. Keep on going until you are happy with the look, then tie off on a nail and cut the string.

Talk about

- What design did you choose and why?
- Was it easy hammering in the nails? What helped?
- Why do you think that Jesus would allow himself to be killed on a cross?

Stained glass

Mess rating 3/5 • Danger rating 1/5 • Difficulty 3/5

Create your own version of stained glass. These will look great at church or at home. Really simple and easy to replace should you want to do different themes each month. Don't be put off by the oil – it's not as messy as it sounds.

Themes

> **God is light** (1 John 1:5–7); **God created light** (Genesis 1:3–4); **Jesus claimed to be the light of the world** (John 8:12); **turning to the light** (John 12:35–36)

Craft outline

You will need

- Roll of art paper or A4 sheets if doing individual ones
- Crayons or oil pastels
- Watercolour paints
- Paintbrushes
- Scissors
- Vegetable oil

Roll out the paper on a table, securing each end so it doesn't roll back up. Use the oil pastels to either draw a Bible scene or just scribble all over it and get your art on. Using the watercolour paints, paint all over the paper, leaving no white paper showing and leave to dry.

When dry, cut up the paper to fit the size of window or windows where you want to display it. Turn the paper over, and on the reverse paint a thin layer all over with the vegetable oil. The oil will make the paper translucent and also help stick the paper to the window.

Talk about

- Can you see the colours shining on other surfaces?
- How does it feel to be surrounded by the coloured light?
- What's your favourite colour?
- Are there stained-glass windows where you are? What stories do they tell?
- Why do you think we describe Jesus as 'light'?

Edible crafts

Edible dirt garden

Mess rating 3/5 • Danger rating 1/5 • Difficulty 2/5

If we're honest, we've probably all eaten dirt at least once in our lives, but you're guaranteed to enjoy this dirt and come back for more. Dads and boys will enjoy this activity as it's not at all 'pretty'.

We served the dirt in terracotta pots but it's your activity, so go wild with it. How about making a whole Easter garden with edible flowers and stones, like the garden at Willy Wonka's chocolate factory?

Themes

Easter; the garden of Eden (Genesis 2:4–15); **the garden of Gethsemane** (Matthew 26:36–46)

Craft outline

You will need

- Cream-filled chocolate cookies
- Chocolate cake
- Shortbread-type biscuits
- Raisins
- Jelly worms
- Desiccated coconut

- Green food colouring
- Rolling pin; ziplock plastic bags; bowls; small terracotta pots for individual servings; lolly sticks

This is an example of a recipe, but, to be honest, as long as the result is tasty and looks like dirt, it's a winner.

Break up the chocolate cake into small lumps and place in the bowl. Put the cream-filled cookies into the ziplock bag, squeeze out the air and seal. Roll the rolling pin over the bag to make fine crumbs. Shake to mix and then add the crumbs to the cake. Do the same with the shortbread to create 'sand' and mix it in with the cookies and cake. Add the raisins, stirring carefully so as to leave some cake lumps.

Put the desiccated coconut into a bag with a few drops of food colouring and shake until it's all green, like grass.

Pile some of the 'dirt' into a terracotta pot and sprinkle on some 'grass'. Write your name or maybe a Bible verse on the lolly stick and poke it into the soil. Add a wiggly jelly worm on top, hanging over the side for a final flourish.

Talk about

- How do you think God created the world?
- Easter and spring time
- What do you like to grow in your garden?
- What's your favourite vegetable?
- Harvest

Curry pastes

Mess rating 3/5 • Danger rating 3/5 • Difficulty 3/5

Going out for a curry remains a hugely popular activity for church groups. Although it would be tricky to make a full curry at a Messy Church, these curry pastes are a great way to get some delicious aromas floating around, and would make for an amazing dinner at home.

Themes

The Holy Spirit; prayer (marinating thoughts and ideas and offering them to God); sharing; friends

Craft outline

You will need

- A selection of different dried spices, including:
  - Dried chillies
  - Paprika or smoked paprika
  - Turmeric
  - Garam masala
  - Cumin seeds
  - Coriander seeds
  - Fenugreek seeds

- o Brown mustard seeds
- o Cayenne pepper
- o Tomato purée
- o Fresh chillies (green and red), coriander, ginger and garlic
- Oil
- Pestle and mortar or small food processor; jars or plastic tubs
- Non-stick frying pan and camping hob

For an authentic recipe, combine the dried spices and toast them gently in the frying pan before you proceed. The smell will be incredible and will definitely add something to your Messy Church. Once toasted, empty the spices into a pestle and mortar or food processor and grind them to a fine powder.

Add around two tablespoons of oil to the mixture, as well as any other ingredients, and continue to grind or blitz until you have a smooth paste.

Spoon the mixture into jars or plastic tubs and take home to cook with meat for a curry. You could, of course, use a specific recipe, but I prefer the creativity of designing your very own curry. You could even try to come up with authentic-sounding names.

Be careful of the heat from the frying pan, and, if you're using fresh chillies, make sure people wash their hands well before rubbing their eyes.

Talk about

- What does the spicy smell make you think of?
- Do you enjoy eating with friends? How about cooking for friends?
- Can you imagine sitting down with Jesus and the disciples for a meal? What do you think they would talk about?

Flat breads

Mess rating 2/5 • Danger rating 3/5 • Difficulty 2/5

There's something satisfying about making bread, and kneading dough is a good physical activity that makes conversation a doddle. These flat breads are really easy to make, without all the bother of waiting for hours for the dough to prove.

You will need to cook the dough in a frying pan over a stove (the compact camping stoves with the gas cartridges are ideal for this), so take real care to make sure no one gets burnt.

Themes

> **Holy Communion; the feeding of the 5,000** (Mark 6:34–44); **the last supper** (Mark 14:22–26)

Craft outline

You will need

- 110 g wholemeal flour
- 50 ml water
- Mixing bowl; rolling pin; frying pan; stove; tongs

Put the flour in a bowl and slowly add water, mixing and kneading until you have a soft, elastic dough. It's best to add the water slowly so that you don't use too much. The longer you knead the dough, the softer the bread will be.

Once the dough is ready, split it into two and roll the pieces into round flat breads, using a rolling pin or the flat of your hand.

Heat the frying pan to a medium heat, and place the bread in it for 20–30 seconds, until the surface starts to bubble. Using the tongs, turn the bread over. Cook for a further 10–15 seconds. The surface of the bread should have brown spots just starting to appear.

Allow the bread to cool slightly and then eat. You can spread with a little butter if you like.

If you prefer to make up a bigger batch of dough, just multiply the quantities accordingly.

Talk about

- Is it hard work kneading the dough?
- What does the smell of the cooking bread remind you of?
- Why do you think Jesus chose to give us bread as a way of remembering him?

Making butter

Mess rating 3/5 • Danger rating 0/5 • Difficulty 1/5

This activity can't help but get everyone's attention, especially when you spread your homemade butter on bread for your Messy tea. It's a physical activity that will require some patience.

Themes

> **Conversion of Paul** (Acts 9:1–19) **and Zacchaeus** (Luke 19:1–10); **Lunch for David's brothers** (1 Samuel 17:17–18); **feeding of the 5,000** (Mark 6:34–44)

Craft outline

You will need

* Lots of double cream; empty jam jars with lids

Half fill your jam jar with cream, carefully seal the lid and then shake the jar for all you're worth. The process takes some time: you'll think it hasn't worked and then, all of a sudden, realise that something has changed. The cream will have separated into butter and but-termilk. Drain the buttermilk away and you're left with a lump of yummy butter.

If you want to go 'gourmet', you can flavour the butter with all sorts of different ingredients: chilli, pepper, fresh herbs or just a sprinkle of sea salt.

Talk about

- How does it feel, waiting for the cream to change? Exciting? Frustrating? Boring?
- The change is quite dramatic: how does it feel to have made your own butter?
- Can you think of stories about people in the Bible who changed dramatically?
- Why does meeting Jesus make such a difference for some people?

Rocky road

Mess rating 2/5 • Danger rating 1/5 • Difficulty 2/5

Chocolate, marshmallows, biscuits and whatever else you fancy putting into these delicious rocky roads – it's food to the extreme.

Themes

> **Roads; journeys; creation; the Emmaus road** (Luke 24:13–33)

Craft outline

You will need

- 125 g butter
- 300 g chocolate (broken)
- 3 tbsp golden syrup
- Broken biscuits
- Mini marshmallows
- Other ingredients to mix in: dried fruit (morello cherries and apricots are really good), bits of sponge cake, meringue, chopped-up chocolate bars, dried chilli flakes, and so on
- Mixing bowls; spoons; bun tin and muffin cases
- Heat source (a microwave is probably safest, but you could use a pan on a hob or a camping stove)
- Fridge or cool place

If you are using a microwave, cube the butter and put it in a micro-waveable bowl with the broken chocolate and the golden syrup. Heat the mixture for 30 seconds at a time, mixing well after each blast. You want the mixture to melt together but not to boil.

If you are working with a hob or stove, heat the same ingredients gently until they melt together.

Let individuals mix together the crunchy and chewy ingredients in their own bowls: be as adventurous as you like. Dried chilli flakes would make a great extreme addition.

Pour some of the chocolate mixture over the other ingredients (enough to bind them together) and then spoon into the muffin cases. Set the rocky roads to cool, and enjoy with tea or package up to take home.

Increase the quantities of butter, chocolate and golden syrup, depending on how much demand you think there may be.

Talk about

- Sometimes life is smooth and sometimes it's rocky: can you think of times when you've experienced both?
- What makes the rocky times easier?
- How does it feel to know that Jesus promises to be always with us?

Tealight s'mores

Mess rating 4/5 • Danger rating 3/5 • Difficulty 2/5

S'mores are an American camping delicacy combining toasted marshmallows, chocolate and biscuits. They're totally delicious, sticky and messy, and, because they involve cooking over a fire, they're totally man-friendly.

Using tealights makes this activity safer than using a barbecue or an open fire, but you do need to be careful to avoid burning. Also remember that you will need to let the marshmallows cool a little before eating. Waiting is such a drag!

Themes

> **The barbecue on the beach** (John 21:9–13); **the pillar of fire and the manna** (Exodus 13:21–22; 16:13–36); **telling stories and sharing the gospel**

Craft outline

You will need

- Biscuits (traditionally, graham crackers, but rich teas or digestives are good); chocolate; marshmallows

- Tealights; long toasting sticks
- A bucket of water

Each person will need two biscuits, a chunk of chocolate and a marshmallow or two on a stick. Toast the marshmallows over the tealight (with close supervision) and, when they are all hot and gooey, make them into a sandwich with the biscuits and the chocolate.

I suggest you have a bucket of water to hand, so that if a marshmallow catches fire you can drop it safely in.

Talk about

- Have you ever had a camp fire? What was it like?
- Do you like telling stories? What about being told stories?
- Can you tell the story of Jesus?

Appendix:
Planning a male-friendly Messy Church

The first way to attract men and boys to your Messy Church is to change their perception of what it will be like. We can think of very few dads who wouldn't want to spend an hour doing messy activities with their children, especially when those activities are organised (and cleaned up) by someone else. In fact, it's pretty much a dream come true for those who, as children, loved playing with Lego™ and Meccano™, remember helping out in workshops with dads, uncles or grandads, and loved doing woodwork and metalwork at school (called Design Technology these days). Dads enjoy coming to our Messy Churches because they know they can race toy cars, build towers, have a go at science experiments, and do all of it with their children.

We're sure that any dads who have ever attended toddler groups and felt like spare parts, and have arrived at Messy Church filled with trepidation, expecting mums and small children to look at them with fear and mistrust, will have been greatly relieved to see the two of us up to our elbows in gunge, sawing, hammering and drilling, or just sitting on the floor reading stories to a small group. They don't necessarily come and talk to us (they are still men, after all), but they do feel that Messy Church might be a place for them.

Having said that men and women, boys and girls are capable of enjoying the same kinds of activities, it is worth noting that men will always struggle with some things; and it's often based more on what we feel others will think of us than on whether we actually want to get involved or not.

Fiddly, 'pretty' activities are unlikely to interest men: they're more likely to go for bending nails into cross shapes than making flowers with quilling paper. This doesn't mean that you should avoid any 'pretty' crafts but it does mean that you need a mixture. Work hard to make sure that for every activity that involves sitting down quietly, there is an alternative that involves moving around and making noise. If you're offering a couple of small paper-based activities, make sure you add in a couple of big 'making things' options as well.

Getting involved

Forgive the stereotype, but picture the man at a children's birthday party. The children are all happily engaged with their activities, the mums are busily setting out food, tidying stuff away or chatting merrily over a brew, and the dad... well, the dad is standing in the corridor, holding a coat and looking awkward.

There are lots of reasons why men don't know how to get involved at a children's event. As Gideon Burrows, author of *Men Can Do It! The real reason dads don't do childcare*, said in a radio interview, it's because they're essentially lazy and because women don't trust them to do things properly. Somehow, lots of men just don't know what their role is at these kinds of events. We're getting better at looking after our own children (although the statistics still say that women do the vast majority of the childcare), but we still feel awkward in situations like Messy Church. Let's try to find a few ways to help men feel more welcome.

One of the main ways to get blokes signed up is to give them a role. Pete has a good friend (not a churchgoer) who looks forward each year to the St Wilfrid's Apple Pick and Chutney Day. Once a year, we get a team of people together to pick all the apples from the two or three trees in the church garden, sort, wash and chop them, and then cook up jars of chutney to sell for church funds. Pete's friend isn't terribly keen on joining in the usual Sunday morning activities of singing and praying, but he loves the teamwork and camaraderie of Apple Day. Blokes like to be involved because, if we have a job, we have a reason to be there.

It's probably fair to say that women are generally better at getting together for a chat, whereas men seem to like to do something together. Don't be frightened to give the dads at your Messy Church a job, or to invite dads who don't usually attend to come and do something. Whether it's running a table, building a catapult, stacking up a tower, leading the singing, reading the Bible or heading up the cooking team, just invite them to get involved and don't forget to invite them back to do it again. Another thing to do, of course, is to hand your dads the theme for the next Messy Church and ask them to come up with a blokey activity to fit it – simple!

Altering people's perceptions is as simple as being careful with the way we promote ourselves. If you have men or dads at your Messy Church, ask them to tell you why they come, and use their thoughts and words in your publicity. Make sure that when you're taking pictures, you include them. Do all you can to get them involved in leading and organising. After you've got to know them a bit, why not organise a blokes' night out to the pub? This is still probably one of the best ways to come up with some ideas and planning and a chance to talk about your faith. Barry's had so many great God-conversations in the pub with other blokes who aren't Christians, and nine times out of ten it was them who started the conversation. Out of church on neutral ground is a great way to get to know the new Messy dad's and for them to get to know you. Barry's church runs a 'Men's Breakfast' at the pub next door on the first Saturday of the month. This is a perfect opportunity to invite the dad's to with minimal organising – day/time/place – sorted!

The celebration time

Don't panic: we're not going to suggest anything too radical. There are, however, a few tweaks you can make that will help men to feel more at ease in your celebration time.

Have blokes telling the story

This is an obvious place to start. If there any dads who enjoy telling stories to their children, invite them to do that as part of your celebration. One of the beauties of the Messy Church celebration is that it's short and broken down into easily defined areas. The story needn't last any longer than four or five minutes, and, done well, it can even be read from a good picture storybook. Dads generally love snuggling down with their kids for a story, and this is just an extension of that activity. If you give a dad lots of encouragement, you're bound to end up with someone who could be part of your team more regularly.

In particular, look for people who speak in front of others regularly as part of their job. Teachers are the obvious choice, but anyone whose work has an element of training will be used to standing in front of others, and anyone who manages other people will also fit that bill.

Live music

Everyone knows that men hate singing. All the books say it. That's why football matches are so quiet, why rock concerts only attract women and why 'Beer and Hymns' at the Greenbelt festival was such an unmitigated disaster. Yes?

Men do like singing, but often they don't like people to hear them singing. If the music at your Messy Church is a bit stilted and quiet, it's only going to create discomfort for everyone. On the other hand, if it's being led by someone with confidence and gusto, people are far more likely to get involved. At Barry's Messy Church in Southampton, a man leads the music on an electric guitar, with a band, and Barry stands at the front and leads the actions with confidence – and no one feels awkward. It means that the singers can sing to their hearts' content and the non-singers are not standing out like sore thumbs, because they're surrounded by noise and activity.

There's something about live music that is always attractive, and lots of the songs that we sing at Messy Church are really simple. Have you got any dads who have a guitar sitting at home that just needs dusting off, or have a secret desire to rekindle their youthful rock star ambitions? A bloke with a guitar leading the song with even the tiniest bit of confidence can be really helpful. And if not a dad then this is also a great opportunity to get any of the teens at your church involved. Have your own Messy Church worship band, give them a role and they'll have a sense of ownership and value and now you have some potential role models for the messy children coming along.

If that's not possible, though, simply think about the kinds of songs you're singing. Are they accessible, with simple language that any-one can engage with? Are they pitched correctly for men's voices? Many Christian worship songs are pitched way too high for the average bloke to sing; men will often stand quietly rather than risk sounding like their former pubescent selves!

You don't need a band, of course. Plenty of music is available on CD for you to sing along with, and you can easily whack the volume up to hide even the most tone-deaf participant. (Pete recommends the Fischy Music CDs as the only child-friendly music that he's happy to listen to in the car – even, occasionally, without his children.)

If your numbers are small and you know that singing is always going to be an issue, just don't do it. You can always use music and video clips instead, which people can watch, listen and respond to. There's absolutely no rule that dictates that worship must involve songs.

Action songs

We're a bit split on this issue. The assumption is that men hate singing and hate action songs even more, but Barry maintains that, led well, with everyone encouraged to take part, action songs can be a real winner for dads. Again, be aware that men are often super-conscious of how others perceive them. While some songs with beautiful Makaton signing might look amazing, a burly bloke may well feel uncomfortable joining in, whereas 'helping a child with big bold actions' is far easier to engage with. It all comes back to encouraging interaction between parent and child.

Banter

Love it or hate it, banter is something distinctly blokey. Stereo-typically, we might struggle to engage in long, emotion-fuelled conversations with our peers, but we're always up for a bit of banter. Make sure that you interact with your congregation during the celebration and create the kind of atmosphere in which they can talk back to you. Part of the genius of the Pixar films, for example, is that they are filled with jokes and comments for the adults. This is one of the reasons they are so successful: they look like children's entertainment, but adults can engage with them too. Don't be frightened about having a little joke with the other grown-ups over the heads of the children.

Adult/parent interaction

A common gripe from Messy Church leaders is that, during the celebration, children sit at the front on the floor and parents sit further back, chatting or looking at their mobile phones. While a bit of banter might overcome that division, be careful to plan celebrations that encourage parent–child interaction. We use the phrase 'in your household groups' over and over again in our celebrations, and we send children back to their mum, dad or carer over and over again. We plan prayer activities and even story activities that mean people have to work together. Like most people, dads will want to be seen to be doing the right thing, so they will often model these kinds of discussions and interactions really well.

Anti-alienation

I tread carefully as I write this! It's important that men don't feel alienated in the Messy Church setting, and this extends beyond the celebration into the rest of your time together. Gideon Burrows, as we've mentioned before, acknowledges that while some of men's hesitation to get engaged with childcare is self-imposed or is simply down to laziness, there is also sometimes the feeling that women don't trust men to get it right. Men, who may already feel uncomfortable in a childcare setting, can be totally alienated by disparaging comments or by having activities taken away from them in order to 'stop them making a mess of it'. We're really conscious that this is contentious stuff, so just bear in mind that men will be as upset by sexist comments or jokes as women would be if the tables were turned. As they are often the minority in Messy Church settings, men should be encouraged as much as possible.

Keep it simple

This final reflection applies to all of our interactions in Messy Church, not just the celebrations: we need to avoid theological overcomplexity in what we communicate. No one likes to feel stupid, so we need to do all we can to prevent that from happening. We need to make sure we avoid churchy language if at all possible, especially when we are dealing with people who are not church regulars. A lot of Christian jargon is so familiar that it often slips into our conversation without us even noticing. We know that men are less likely to attend church than women, so we need to assume that those who are at our Messy Church will feel alienated by language that isn't deliberately inclusive. Don't be frightened of breaking things down in order to be better understood: I'd rather share an oversimplified explanation, which makes someone want to know more, than switch them off by assuming too much and using overly complex language.

What next?

If you have men who are starting to attend Messy Church more regularly, it's worth exploring how to spend some more time with them, to make opportunities for building better relationships.

At Barry's church, there is a regular men's group that meets for a variety of different activities. They've been on weekends away together, walking and climbing, and have watched films together (*Senna* was particularly good, as it brought up some good discussions about faith). There is usually curry, and beer features highly too. And not forgetting the monthly 'Men's Breakfast' where life chat, a full English and unlimited refillable coffee are matched perfectly. Most of these are organised under the men's group name of '3G – Guys, God & Grub'. Named as a bit of fun and to help advertise in the church news sheet but also because as a bloke I think we all want to belong to something where we can fit in and be ourselves.

At Pete's church, they are pursuing a more all-age approach, and, following on from Messy Church, there is now a regular monthly all-age home group that meets on Saturday mornings for bacon butties, coffee and newspapers, followed by a chance to read the Bible together and pray. It's still in its infancy, but Messy Café hopes to include occasional family outings together – stuff that men will find attractive, but with their children too.

All men are different, and what works for us in Cowplain and Bitterne may not work for you in your setting. For every bloke who likes beer and rugby, there will be another who prefers reading and walking. Just as there is no one catch-all activity for children or women, the same is true for men.

Ultimately, you need to take the plunge and give it a go. Probably, engaging with the dads and asking them what they'd like to do is the best place to start.

As I finish writing this edition it's June 2020 and we are in the Covid-19 lockdown – hopefully near the end, but that is yet to be known. It feels a little odd to be writing a book about Messy Church while we can't actually run one in our churches. It's in God's hands and we must trust in him to guide us through. The last 'proper' Messy Church we ran inside church was in February 2020. My church, like many, closed its doors temporarily in March a week before our next Messy Church.

I've seen other churches run 'virtual' Messy Churches and send out activity sheets to keep in contact with their Messy families. Here at Holy Saviour Bitterne we've also run 'Bearded Barry's Church TV' (BBCTV) on Facebook Live every Monday to Thursday, playing games, reading Bible stories, craft activities, sharing jokes and pictures that have been emailed in and interacting with our Messy families as well as amazingly folk in Essex, Wales, California and Australia watching live. It's been really interesting to see how many dads have been watching with their children and joining in on the games and sending in jokes. They've been doing church but in the comfort of their own home, without any pressure. I look forward to the chats we will have in the future face to face.

It's been such a blessing to be able to do it and has made me think how our Messy Church will look when our doors are back open and we can return. It will be different, I'm sure of it. Not because what we used to do was wrong but because we've learnt new things from adapting to lockdown. We will certainly be keeping up with the Facebook Live shows, perhaps once a month to start with. One thing for certain is that we'll still be trying to get the dads along and feeling part of something they can belong to and own without feeling uncomfortable.

Barry Brand

is the children and youth minister at Holy Saviour Bitterne and
has run a large Messy Church since 2012. He's constantly being
encouraged to tidy up his office, which is full of cardboard tubes
and other potential craft materials that will be useful 'one day'.
He's written for the *Get Messy!* magazine and was part of the team
for the Messy International Conference 2019. Barry is married to
Adele, with two children, George and Freddie, who are part of the
team at Messy Church helping on the craft tables or playing in the
band. Outside of church he enjoys cycling, camping and eating
with friends, and is a keen cook who, much to Adele's dismay,
uses far more pots than necessary.

Pete Maidment

works as the lay chaplain at Lord Wandsworth College in
Hampshire, where he teaches Religious Studies, coaches hockey
(badly) and runs the Saturday morning BBQ club. He is a mental
health first aid trainer and is a passionate advocate for young
people's mental health and well-being. He was part of the Messy
Church core team at St Wilfrid's Church, Cowplain, and does his
best to inject some of that creativity into his weekly whole-school
assemblies. Pete is married with two children, both at secondary
school.